ODDBALLS

THE GRAPHIC NOVEL

New Stories. Same Mayhem.

ODDBALLS

New York Times bestselling author
JAMES RALLISON
and ETHAN BANVILLE

A TARCHERPERIGEE BOOK

tarcherperigee

AN IMPRINT OF PENGUIN RANDOM HOUSE LLC
penguinrandomhouse.com

Trade paperback ISBN: 9780593543474
Ebook ISBN: 9780593543481

Printed in the United States of America
1st Printing

Composition by Lorie Pagnozzi

THIS BOOK IS DEDICATED TO ALL THE PEOPLE WHO PREFER READING GRAPHIC NOVELS OVER TRADITIONAL BOOKS. WE GET YOU. WE WANT SOMETHING PRETTY TO LOOK AT TOO.

ODDBALLS

LONGEST YARDSALE

C'MON, JAMES!!!!!

NO TICKET, NO SLIDE.
ROXANNE, MY FRIEND, CAN'T YOU MAKE AN EXCEPTION JUST THIS ONCE?
LIFEGU
BUT ONLY FOR ME. DON'T WANT ANY OTHER FREELOADERS, AM I RIGHT?
EG
LIFEGU
NO TICKET, NO SLIDE.

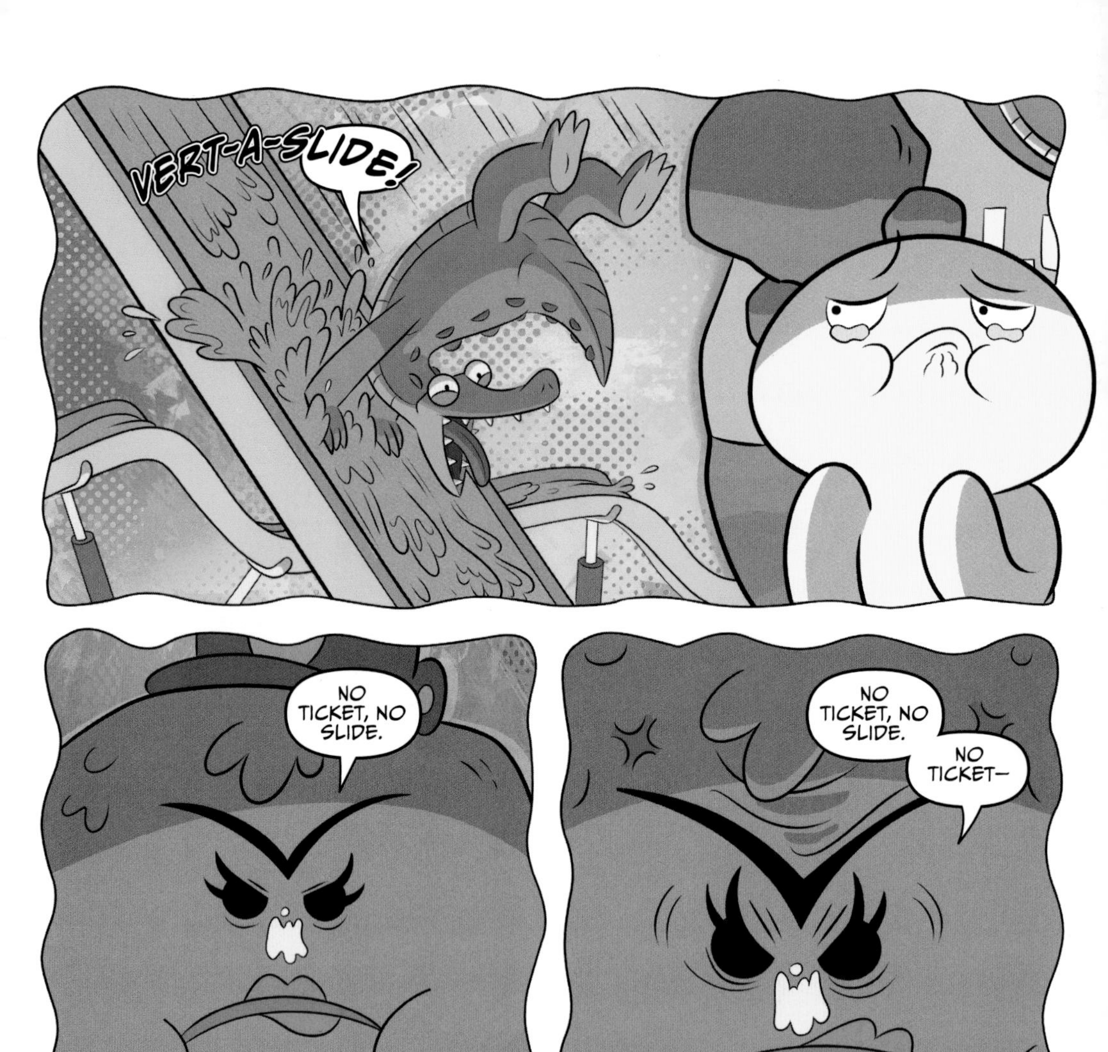
VERT-A-SLIDE!
NO TICKET, NO SLIDE.
NO TICKET, NO SLIDE.
NO TICKET—

NO SLIDE!!!

OH. IT WAS JUST A DREAM.

WAIT. THEN WHY IS MY BED FLOODED?

SQUELCH
SQUELCH
SQUELCH

SQUIRT SQUIRT SQUIRT

MAX! WHAT ARE YOU DOING?
I HEARD YOU HAVING A NIGHTMARE AND WANTED TO MAKE SURE YOU GOT TO FEEL THE EXPERIENCE OF THE SLIDE YOU WEREN'T GETTING TO RIDE!

WAIT, YOU COULD SEE WHAT I WAS DREAMING?
SURE! IT'S A CROC THING.

WAIT . . . DID YOU SEE WHAT I DREAMT THE OTHER—
DINING WITH SPIDERS?! YOU NEED HELP, MAN!
BUT WE'VE GOT MORE IMPORTANT THINGS TO WORRY ABOUT, LIKE YOU NOT HAVING MONEY TO GO TO GUSHING MEADOWS AND RIDE THE VERT-A-SLIDE!

HOW'D YOU KNOW I DON'T HAVE MONEY FOR THE WATER PARK? THAT A CROC THING TOO?
NOPE. I'M JUST FAMILIAR WITH YOUR HISTORY OF FREELOADING.

YOU SAY THAT AS IF IT'S A BAD THING, BUT I'VE MADE IT THROUGH MY ENTIRE CHILDHOOD MANIPULATING PEOPLE TO PAY FOR MY EVERYTHING.
I'M ON A ROLL, MAX.
NOT SURE THAT'S SOMETHING TO BE PROUD OF.
I'M GONNA ADD THAT TO MY LIST OF THINGS YOU NEED HELP WITH.

WELL, WHILE YOU WORK ON YOUR LIST OF PARTS OF ME THAT I'LL NEVER CHANGE, I'LL GO WORK MY PARENTS FOR MONEY!
FLUMP

MOM, DAD, THIS IS THE MOST IMPORTANT THING I'M EVER GOING TO ASK–
NOPE.

BUT YOU DON'T KNOW WHAT I WAS GOING TO ASK FOR!
LET ME GUESS, IT STARTS WITH "MON" AND ENDS WITH "EY."
YOU WANT A MONKEY?
PHEW! I THOUGHT YOU WANTED MONEY.
MOM, I DON'T WANT MONEY. I NEED MONEY. IN FACT, I THINK I'M OWED MONEY. MY ALLOWANCE!
SORRY, HONEY. YOU HAVEN'T DONE ANY OF YOUR CHORES.

HA! HA HA!
WHAT ARE YOU TALKING ABOUT? I'VE BEEN CRUSHING THE CHORE CHART.

SEE? I TOOK CARE OF HAMMY!
Weekly Chores
MOW LAWN
WASH DISHES
HELP WITH LAUNDRY
CLEAN ROOM
FEED HAMSTER

NO, YOU "SET HIM FREE TO LIVE AS HAMSTERS WERE SUPPOSED TO LIVE."

AN ALLOWANCE IS JUST A MEANS FOR PARENTS TO EXERT CONTROL OVER THEIR CHILDREN!
GIVING TOKEN AMOUNTS OF MONEY EVERY TWO WEEKS TO KEEP US CONTENT ENOUGH THAT WE WON'T OVERTHROW OUR PARENTS' TYRANNICAL RULE!
WELL, THE WORLD ALWAYS NEEDS PAPER-BOYS. YOU COULD EARN MONEY THAT WAY.

PAPERBOYS?! NO ONE READS NEWSPAPERS. THIS ISN'T 2014, DAD!
HONEY, YOUR DAD WORKS WITH OLD ROCKS ALL DAY; HE DOESN'T KNOW WHAT YEAR IT IS.

MOOOOOOOM? PLEASE!
LOOK, YOUR DAD AND I ARE GOING TO A MATINEE OF THAT NEW ROCK OPERA.

DEED-ILY DEED-ILY MWOW MWOW
THAT LOOKS AWFUL!

IF YOU CAN FIND A JOB AND EARN THE MONEY, YOU CAN GO WITH MAX TO THE WATER PARK TODAY.
BUT THAT'S IMPOSSIBLE!
CHEER UP, PAL!
IF YOU DON'T WANT TO GET A JOB, YOU CAN MAKE A WATER PARK IN THE FRONT YARD!
SEE? INSTANT WATER PARK!
HAVE FUN, HONEY! AND DON'T FORGET TO TURN THE HOSE OFF WHEN YOU'RE DONE!
PLAP
CAN YOU BELIEVE THAT, MAX? I WANT TO RIDE THE VERT-A-SLIDE AND I GET THIS—IT'S COMPLETELY HORIZONTAL!
NOBODY WANTS SOME CHEAP, FRONT-YARD, HORIZONTAL WATER PARK, DO THEY, MAX?

I'M SLIIIIDIIIINNNG!
SLIP-SLIDING ON A SUNNY DAY! MIND IF I JOIN?
OOO. YAAAY. FUH-UHN.
NO! NO ENJOYMENT OF THIS!
HSS
HSSSSSS
PLAP
HAWWHUMP
I'VE HAD ENOUGH OF MY PARENTS CONTROLLING ME WITH MONEY, MAX. I'M GOING TO TAKE CONTROL.
YOU'RE GONNA DO THE RESPONSIBLE THING AND GET A JOB?!

HA! COULD YOU IMAGINE?
NO. I'M NOT BREAKING MY FREELOADING STREAK. YOU'RE GOING TO SELL MY JUNK AT A YARD SALE!
AW, HECK YEAH!
WAIT. YOU PROMISED TO LEAVE ME YOUR JUNK IN YOUR WILL!
SORRY, MAX. BUT IF WE WANT TO EXPERIENCE THE INTENSE WEDGIE YOU GET FROM THE VERT-A-SLIDE, SACRIFICES MUST BE SOLD.

SOON . . .
POOPSY WHOOPS & KITTY The CARNIVAL
Pogo Mahn

EXCUSE ME, JAMES. HOW MUCH IS THIS POGO MAHN GLASS? I'M HOPING SOMEDAY TO HAVE A FRIEND OVER AND WANT TO BE PREPARED.
SORRY, MR. MCFLY, BUT ANSWERING QUESTIONS WILL MAKE THIS FEEL LIKE A JOB, AND I'M NOT DOING THIS FOR A JOB.
I'M DOING THIS FOR THE MONEY.

WELL, THEN HOW ABOUT TWO DOLLARS?
FORM OF A STATEMENT, PLEASE.

HERE'S TWO DOLLARS.
MAX WILL RING YOU UP.

MAX?

I TOLD YOU, MAN, IT'S NOT FOR SALE!

MAX, BUDDY, I KNOW YOU WERE PLANNING ON INHERITING ALL THIS, BUT NOTHING IS OFF-LIMITS IN THIS YARD SALE IF IT'LL GET ME TO THE WATER PARK.
SO, WHAT ARE WE SELLING? OLD MAGAZINES? VHSs? EXPIRED SNOW GLOBES?

HE WANTS TO BUY YOUR YARD, MAN!

HI, I'M BYRON B. SELLERS.
I COULDN'T HELP BUT NOTICE THIS GREAT FOUNDATION— I MEAN, YARD—THAT YOU HAVE FOR SALE.

I KNOW WHO YOU ARE, SELLERS. HOW MUCH YOU OFFERING?
BUT, JAMES! IT'S YOUR YARD!

YEP, AND IT'S GONNA BE SELLERS'S YARD IF IT'LL GET ME ON THE VERT-A-SLIDE.
SMART INVESTMENT. NOTHING HOLDS ITS VALUE MORE THAN MEMORIES OF PLUMMETING DOWN A SLIDE OF WATER SUPERCHARGED WITH THE SCREAMS OF CHILDREN.

I'M OFFERING FIVE HUNDRED DOLLARS . . . CASH.
SOLD!
PLEASURE DOING BUSINESS WITH YOU.

OKAY, PEOPLE, THE SALE'S OVER!

HSS HSSS
YIPE

SEE, MAX? TOLD YOU I'D GET MONEY FOR THE WATER PARK.
BUT WON'T YOUR PARENTS KILL YOU WHEN THEY FIND OUT YOU SOLD THEIR YARD?

NOTHING'S GOING TO HAPPEN TO MY FRONT YARD, SO MY PARENTS WILL BE NONE THE WISER.
YOU SEE, MAX, THE ONLY REASON FRONT YARDS EXIST IS TO PUT A LITTLE DISTANCE BETWEEN ONE'S HOUSE AND THE PEOPLE ON THE SIDEWALK.
THE "SIDEWALKERS," IF YOU WILL.

NO ONE WANTS TO BE NEAR THE SIDEWALKERS, SO SELLERS JUST GAVE ME FIVE HUNDRED DOLLARS FOR LAND THAT IS ESSENTIALLY USELESS, BECAUSE ANYTHING HE DOES HERE WILL BE TOO CLOSE TO THE WALKERS.
HMM. IT SOUNDS LOGICAL, BUT IT ALSO SOUNDS LIKE YOU'RE MAKING EXCUSES TO JUSTIFY YOUR IRRESPONSIBLE AND SELFISH ACTIONS.

IRRESPONSIBLE ACTIONS THAT ARE GETTING US TO THE WATER PARK!
I NEVER THOUGHT OF IT THAT WAY!

NOW COME ON. LET'S GO BATHING SUIT SHOPPING.
UNLIKE STORES, PUBLIC LIBRARIES, AND SCHOOLS, THE WATER PARK APPARENTLY REQUIRES CLOTHING.
A LITTLE LATER . . .
I CAN'T BELIEVE YOU SPENT ALMOST ALL YOUR MONEY ON THOSE SUPERB SHORTS.
I SAVED ENOUGH FOR A TICKET. AND IF I HAVE TO PUT CLOTHES ON, I WANNA LOOK GOOD.
SUPERB

SPEAKING OF WHICH, I DON'T THINK A SWIM CAP COUNTS AS CLOTHING, MAX.
THE WATER PARK RULES SAY, "SWIM WEAR REQUIRED."
IT'S A SWIM CAP! "SWIM'S" RIGHT IN THE NAME!
GUSHING MEADOWS

HUH, I COULD HAVE SWORN THIS WAS OUR STREET.
IT IS. THERE'S MY HOUSE!

YOU SURE?
YEP. MY PARENTS ARE CHANGING THE LOCKS AGAIN!

GLUG

SHOVE

HUH.
DON'T OVER PAY FOR SPACE
LIVE IN A LUXURY MICRO HOME

OH NO! WHEN YOUR PARENTS SEE THIS, YOU'RE DEAD! AND I DON'T WANT TO THINK ABOUT CORPSES WHEN I GO TO THE WATER PARK!
UNLESS I GET TO INHERIT ALL YOUR JUNK AGAIN. THEN I COULD GET OVER THE WATER-SLIDING CORPSES.
MY PARENTS CAN'T KILL ME, MAX. BECAUSE IT'S THEIR FAULT.
CAN'T . . . ADMIT FAULT . . . EVER.
MY MOM TOLD ME I COULD GO TO THE WATER PARK IF I EARNED THE MONEY, AND I DID. SHE SHOULD BE PROUD.
THINGS JAMES NEEDS HELP WITH!
OKAY, I'M ABOUT TO HIT YOU WITH THIS NOTEBOOK.
FINE, I'LL BUY THE YARD BACK FROM SELLERS.
WITH WHAT? YOU SPENT ALL BUT $50 ON YOUR DESIGNER TRUNKS!
IT'S CALLED NEGOTIATION, MAX.
SUPERB

HI! INTERESTED IN MOVING INTO THIS LOVELY NEIGHBORHOOD?
I ALREADY LIVE HERE.

THAT'S RIGHT. MANIFEST IT INTO EXISTENCE.
I SOLD YOU MY YARD, SELLERS!
PAT
PAT

BUUUT IT TURNS OUT I "FORGOT" TO TELL YOU ABOUT SOME ISSUES THAT MAY MAKE YOU REGRET BUYING.
IS THAT SO?

YEAH. NOT SURE HOW IT SLIPPED MY MIND. SEE, THIS GROUND'S RIDDLED WITH PRAIRIE DOGS, AND UNDERGROUND METHANE STREAMS . . . AND DON'T EVEN GET ME STARTED ON THE NUCLEAR WASTE . . .

BUT THE GOOD NEWS IS I'M WILLING TO BUY IT BACK. HOW'S ABOUT WE SAY AN EVEN FIFTY BUCKS?

HA! COULD YOU IMAGINE?
BUT NO.
YOU CALL THAT NEGOTIATING?!
SELLERS. I NEED MY YARD BACK.
WELL I CAN'T DO THAT.
BUT IF IT'LL MAKE YOU FEEL BETTER, I'LL LET YOU BE THE FIRST TO RENT ONE OF MY LUXURY MICRO HOMES.
FIRST MONTH IS FREE!
JUST LIKE IT'S FREE FROM SIDEWALKERS, BECAUSE I'M MAKING THEM MY TENANTS!
THE BUILDING EVEN HAS A POOL ON TOP, WITH A WATER SLIDE.
A WATER SLIDE?! IS IT HORIZONTAL?!
YOU KNOW WHAT, SELLERS?
I'LL TAKE IT.

WELCOME TO YOUR NEW HOME!

YOU SURE THIS ISN'T A CLOSET?
NO, I'M NOT.
BATHROOM IS OUT THE BACK AND INSIDE SOME KID'S HOUSE. THEIR ALARM CODE IS 0514. JUST DON'T TRIP OVER THE GARDEN HOSE.

GOOD IDEA, MOVING OUT BEFORE YOUR PARENTS GET HOME. MMHMM.
SHAVE YOUR HEAD, START A NEW LIFE.

WHAT'S YOUR NEW NAME GOING TO BE?
OO, I KNOW. JAMESY! NO, TOO HARD TO REMEMBER.
I'M NOT CHANGING WHO I AM, MAX. THE WORLD WOULD BE LOST WITHOUT MY CHARMS.
SLING

BOOM
SCREEEEEECH
CRASSSHHH

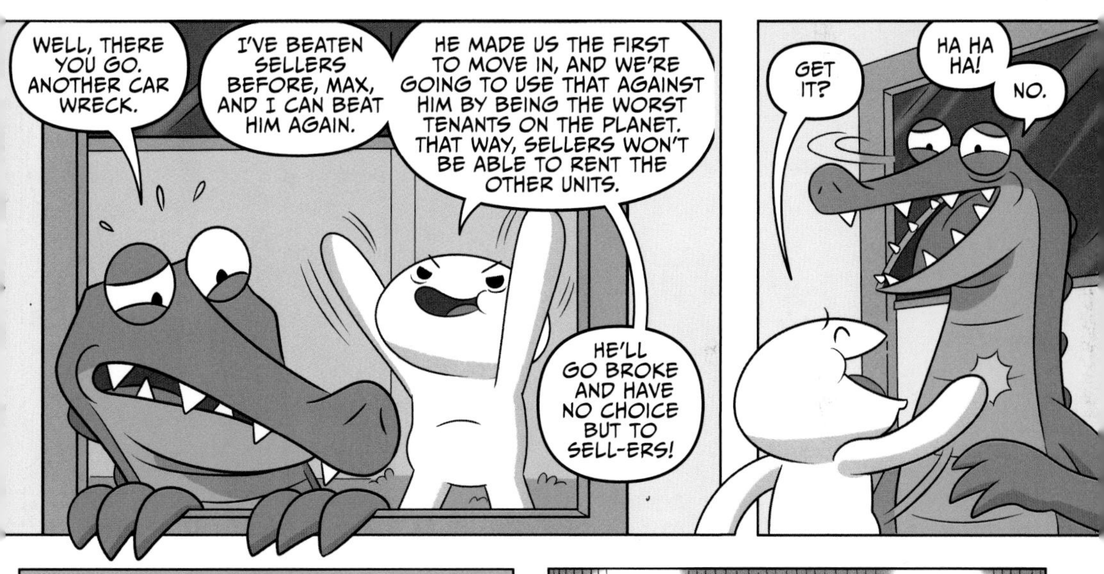
WELL, THERE YOU GO. ANOTHER CAR WRECK.
I'VE BEATEN SELLERS BEFORE, MAX, AND I CAN BEAT HIM AGAIN.
HE MADE US THE FIRST TO MOVE IN, AND WE'RE GOING TO USE THAT AGAINST HIM BY BEING THE WORST TENANTS ON THE PLANET. THAT WAY, SELLERS WON'T BE ABLE TO RENT THE OTHER UNITS.
HE'LL GO BROKE AND HAVE NO CHOICE BUT TO SELL-ERS!
GET IT?
HA HA HA!
NO.

DOESN'T MATTER. PLAY THIS.
BUT, JAMES, I DON'T KNOW HOW TO PLAY A TUBA!

GOOD.

HUHT
HAHT
HO
HEYYY

THIS'LL SEND THAT RENTER RUNNING FOR A QUIETER PLACE TO RUIN.

BUH BUH BUH
PLLLLFFFFT
SCREEEEE

BLART PFFFT FRMP
HUHT HAHT HO HEYYY

HUHT
HAHT
HO
HEYYY

HUHT
HAHT
HO
HEYYY

LOBBY
AS LONG AS I CAN SQUAT ANYTIME I WANT, I'M A HAPPY PERSON!

SORRY, WE JUST STARTED.

LIVE, LAUGH, SQUAT!

HURK!

WITH THIS ELEVATOR I CAN FINALLY ENJOY LIVING WITH A VIEW!

SHOVE
VRRRR
TOLD YOU ROXANNE COULDN'T TAKE THE STAIRS!
VRRRR

PFF

MMM! THANKS TO YOU TWO, NOW I WON'T HAVE TO STOP FOR LUNCH, WHICH MEANS I CAN RENT TO MORE WALKERS!

BUT FIRST—!
OOF!

HEY! YOU CAN'T JUST KICK US OUT!

OH, BUT I CAN.
YOUR LEASE CLEARLY STATES THAT IF I HAVE TO FOIL YOUR ATTEMPTS TO UNDERMINE ME THREE OR MORE TIMES, YOU ARE OUT.
DUE TO THE RULE OF THREES IN COMEDY, I HAVE LEGAL CLEARANCE.

YOU REALLY PUT THAT IN THERE?
NICE PLAYING WITH YOU AGAIN.

NOW WE'VE GOT NO CHANCE OF EXPERIENCING ANY KIND OF WATER SLIDE.
HORIZONTAL, VERTICAL, OR INTER-DIMENSIONAL.
I'M SORRY, MAX. I SHOULD HAVE JUST SETTLED FOR MY DAD'S BUDGET WATER PARK.
GUSHING MEADOWS

GUESS YOUR PARENTS WILL BE HOME SOON. WHAT BORDERLINE CRAZY AND NOT REMOTELY POSSIBLE LIE ARE YOU GOING TO TELL THEM?
I'M NOT GONNA LIE, MAX. IT'S TIMES LIKE THESE WHEN A KID HAS TO TAKE RESPONSIBILITY AND OWN UP TO THEIR ACTIONS.

RIGHT AFTER I GET WHAT I DESERVE.

AAGH!
HEY! OW!
WHAT THE HECK, MAN?!
TWACK
WHUMP
WHACK

WHAT? YOU SAID "WHAT YOU DESERVED"!
I DESERVE A WATER SLIDE, MAX. A WATER SLIDE!
AND I'M NOT GOING TO SPEND THE REST OF MY LIFE GROUNDED WITHOUT EXPERIENCING EVEN A MEDIOCRE ONE.

SO, WHAT'S THE PLAN? CLIMB UP THE SIDE LIKE A GIANT GORILLA, EAT SOME PEOPLE, THEN GO FOR A DIP?
WHAT? NO. THIS ISN'T AN '80s VIDEO GAME, MAX.
JUST FOLLOW MY LEAD.

HEY, WALKERS! SELLERS IS GIVING OUT FREE FISH TACOS WITH A TOUR!

YOU KNOW THAT DOESN'T MAKE IT COME ANY FASTER.
I'M PRETTY SURE IT DOES.
CLK
CLK
CLK
CLK
CLK
MAYBE WE CAN ASK MR. SELLERS!
AGH!
IT ISN'T THE VERT-A-SLIDE WE'D HOPED FOR, MAX, BUT IT'LL STILL MAKE US EXTREMELY MOIST!

SORRY.
NO RENTAL, NO RIDE.
WAIT, ARE YOU A CROCODILE? OR CAN SLIMY SALESMEN SEE DREAMS TOO?
TIME TO GO, FELLAS.
RUMBLE
CRK

YAAAAAAHHH!
CRRRRUMBLE
CRUMP

SSPLASSSHHHH
HAHA!
MOVE OVER VERT-A-SLIDE, HELLO WATER FREE-FALL SLIDE!
MY BUILDING! WHAT HAPPENED?
MAYBE IT WAS THOSE PRETEND PRAIRIE DOGS WHO ANSWERED OUR PRAYERS!

NO, MAX. IT WAS MY COMPLETE LACK OF RESPONSIBILITY.
GUESS LEAVING THE HOSE RUNNING SOFTENED THE GROUND SO MUCH IT CREATED A SINKHOLE!
GURGL
A FRONT-YARD BUILDING CAN WORK, BUT YOU CAN'T HAVE A FRONT-YARD POOL! THE SIDEWALKERS WON'T LEAVE YOU ALONE!

MR. SELLERS! YOU BUILT A POOL?
NO! WALKERS!
BACK! BACK!
TEEHEE HEE HEE HEE!
I'M RUINED!
WOW, SOUNDS LIKE YOU'RE IN A REAL BIND.
TELL YOU WHAT, I'LL BUY IT OFF YOU FOR . . . FIFTY BUCKS.
SNATCH!
HAVE FUN WITH THE WALKERS!
WELL, MAX. I THINK IT'S OFFICIALLY TIME TO BURN YOUR "THINGS JAMES NEEDS HELP WITH" LIST. CLEARLY, I'M PERFECT!
MMM, I FEEL LIKE WE'RE FORGETTING AN IMPORTANT PLOT POINT.
JAMES!

WHAT DID YOU DO TO OUR FRONT YARD?!
WHAT YOU TOLD ME TO DO?
I FOUND A WAY TO EARN MONEY, SELLING REAL ESTATE. I SOLD OUR YARD, LET SOMEONE DEVELOP IT, THEN BOUGHT IT BACK FOR A PROFIT.
OH . . . WELL . . . THAT'S ACTUALLY IMPRESSIVE.
JAMES? YOU BUILT US A POOL?!
CANNON ROCK!
SPLASHH
SO . . . I'M NOT IN TROUBLE?
NOT AT THE MOMENT.
BUT IF YOUR FATHER DOESN'T COME UP FOR AIR IN THE NEXT FIVE MINUTES, LET ME KNOW.

UHH, WE'RE NOT MOVING. ARE WE GONNA GO DOWN?
I THINK THIS IS A FREEZE-FRAME.
THE END

JSMR

I'LL TELL YOU, MAX: THERE'S NOTHING MORE SATISFYING THAN GETTING UP IN FRONT OF A BUNCH OF PEOPLE WHO HAVE NO INTEREST IN HEARING YOU SING AND FORCING THEM TO LISTEN TO YOU SING!

ALL RIGHT, EVERYONE, SETTLE DOWN, SETTLE DOWN. I KNOW YOU'RE ALL EXCITED TO TAKE THIS STANDARDIZED TEST.
I'M HOPING EVERYONE DOES WELL SO WE GET ENOUGH FUNDING AND I CAN FINALLY START GETTING A *PAYCHECK!*

MR. MCFLY! I TOLD YOU, CRAFT SUPPLIES COME FIRST!
BUT IF EVERYONE'S COME PREPARED, I THINK YOU'VE GOT A GOOD CHANCE OF BEING PAID MONEY MADE OUT OF CONSTRUCTION PAPER!
THAT'S STILL ONE STEP CLOSER TO A *REAL PAYDAY!*

OKAY, EVERYONE: TAKE OUT YOUR NUMBER 2 PENCILS.

SQUIRCH SQUELCH

JAMES, DO YOU HAVE THE PENCIL YOU WERE TOLD TO BRING FOR THE TEST CARDS?

I'VE GOT A SLIGHTLY CHEWED PEN . . .

HAD A PEN.

OH NO. NO PENCIL MEANS YOU WON'T BE ABLE TO TAKE THE TEST, WHICH MEANS OUR AVERAGE WILL PLUMMET AND . . .

I GUESS PIGGY WILL HAVE TO WAIT TO BE FED ANOTHER DAY.

BOO HOO HOO!
BOOO! JAMES HURT OUR PATHETIC TEACHER'S FEELINGS!
AND NOT IN A PLAYFUL WAY! HE CRUSHED HIS *SPIRIT!*

BOOOOOOO!
WAIT! THIS ISN'T MY FAULT!

IT'S NOT? I'M PRETTY SURE IT IS.

THIS IS ***STANDARDIZED TESTING'S*** FAULT!

STANDARDIZED TESTING IS A ONE-SIZE-FITS-ALL TEST FOR STUDENTS WHO ARE ALL ***TOTALLY DIFFERENT!***
HOW COULD THAT **EVER** BE SUCCESSFUL?

LIKE, I'M NOT A PENCIL GUY. SO SHOULD I BE FORCED INTO COMPLYING AND BETRAY WHO I AM?
AND WHAT ABOUT THE PRESSURE IT PUTS ON STUDENTS TO PERFORM?

DO YOU KNOW THE ANXIETY IT CAUSES STUART, KNOWING HE'LL LET THE SCHOOL DOWN BECAUSE MATH ISN'T HIS STRONG SUIT?
BUT ONLY BECAUSE IF I'M GOOD AT IT I'LL WANT TO BEAT ***MYSELF*** UP!

AND WHAT ABOUT NEANDER?

HE'S SO SMART THESE TESTS ARE BENEATH HIM!

NEANDER SHOULD BE CHALLENGED BY EXAMS, NOT TURN HIMSELF INTO THE TYPE OF STUDENT WHO FITS INTO SOME BUREAUCRAT'S PENCIL-FILLED **BOX!**

I THINK THEY'RE CIRCLES.
NOT NOW, MAX.

I SAY WE PUT AN **END** TO STANDARDIZED TESTING SO THAT ALL STUDENTS CAN BE THEMSELVES AND LEARN AT THEIR OWN PACE!
IT'S TIME TO SHARE OUR **REAL** FEELINGS ABOUT WANTING A **REAL** EDUCATION, NOT SOME UNIVERSAL ABOMINATION!

DESTROY IT ALL! MY LIFE'S WORK IS A LIE!

I THINK I MADE MY POINT.

SMASH

JAMES, TO MY OFFICE, NOW!

JAMES, YOUR RANTS HAVE CAUSED DESTRUCTION FOR THE LAST TIME.

DUE TO INCITING A SCHOOL UPRISING, PERSUADING STUDENTS TO REFUSE TO TAKE A TEST, AND IN TURN ROBBING THIS SCHOOL OF MUCH-NEEDED FUNDING, YOU ARE HEREBY ***EXPELLED!***

BWAAHA HAHAHAAAAAA!
BUT IF I'M EXPELLED, I'LL BE GROUNDED, AND MAX AND I WON'T GET TO DO ***KARAOKE—***

PLEASE, PRINCIPAL CLOUDSPEAKER—
IT'S ***LOUD-SPEAKER!***

HUH, THAT MAKES MORE SENSE.
PLEASE DON'T EXPEL ME. JUST GIVE ME ANOTHER CHANCE AND I'LL NEVER RANT EVER AGAIN!!
. . .

OKAY. I'LL GIVE YOU A SECOND CHANCE.

WHAT? *REALLY?*
WHY?
BECAUSE SOMEONE ONCE GAVE ***ME*** A SECOND CHANCE.

SEE, BEFORE I WAS PRINCIPAL LOUDSPEAKER, I WAS A SPEAKER THAT BROKE ALL THE RULES.

WHICH IS HOW I ENDED UP AS A LOUDSPEAKER IN DIRT'S JUVENILE HALL.

BUT I WAS GIVEN A SECOND CHANCE TO TURN MY LIFE AROUND.
I WORKED HARD AND I WAS EVENTUALLY PROMOTED TO RUN A MORE *PRISTINE* PRISON:
SCHOOL!

WHICH IS HOW I'M HERE TODAY, ABLE TO GIVE *YOU* A SECOND CHANCE. SO, NO EXPULSION.

BUT REMEMBER, JAMES—I CAN POP UP IN *ANY* SPEAKER, *ANYWHERE.* I'LL BE WATCHING.

NO MORE RANTING!
NO PROBLEM.

YOU—
—JAMES—
—ARE GOING TO **STOP RANTING?**
I KNOW, I KNOW.
RANTING IS WHO I AM. IT'S HOW I EXPRESS MYSELF AND TRY AND INFLUENCE CHANGE.
BUT SOMETIMES YOU HAVE TO BE AN ADULT AND MAKE HARD DECISIONS IN LIFE, ECHO.
WHICH IS WHAT I'M DOING NOW, SO MAX AND I CAN GO TO KARAOKE KIDS' NIGHT.
SO, IF I WERE TO TELL YOU I LIKE PINEAPPLE ON PIZZA, YOU'D HAVE NOTHING TO SAY ABOUT IT.
WHAT?!? PINEAPPLE IS A **TROPICAL FRUIT,** NOT SOME—
I MEAN, **NOPE.**
I SEE NOTHING WRONG WITH THAT.
HMM. MAYBE THIS WILL BE GOOD.
WHILE YOU'RE TOTALLY BETRAYING WHO YOU ARE AS A PERSON, AT LEAST I WON'T HAVE TO ALWAYS BE WATCHING YOUR BACK, KEEPING AN EYE OUT FOR SNIPERS, VENGEFUL MOBS, OR ANGRY APPARITIONS FROM THE SPIRIT REALM.

HERE'S YOUR BANANA SPLIT SUNDAE.
SNAP
SOMETHING WRONG, JAMES?

NO, NO. IT'S JUST . . .
. . . THAT'S NOT A BANANA SPLIT SUNDAE.

BUT THERE'S A BANANA.
YES. BUT I ORDERED A BANANA SPLIT, AND THAT BANANA IS WHOLE.
SEE WHAT I MEAN?

WHAT?
YOU CAN'T CALL IT A SPLIT AND NOT DO THE SPLITTING.

BUT AREN'T YOU GONNA, LIKE, SPLIT IT EVERY TIME YOU TAKE A BITE?
SO YOU WANT ME, THE CUSTOMER, TO DO YOUR JOB FOR YOU?!?
JAMES?

DID I JUST HEAR YOU SLIGHTLY RAISE YOUR VOICE IN THE FORM OF A *QUESTION?*
UH, NO. EVERYTHING'S FINE, PRINCIPAL LOUDSPEAKER.

SO, YOU GONNA, LIKE, SPLIT YOUR OWN SUNDAE, OR WHAT?

"YOU CAN'T SERVE SOMETHING THAT DOESN'T MATCH THE DESCRIPTION. IT'S FALSE ADVERTISING."

AND YOU CAN'T JUST HAND THE WORK OVER TO THE CUSTOMER BECAUSE YOU'RE TOO UNOBSERVANT TO MAKE IT MATCH.
ZZZZZ
SPLAT

JUST BECAUSE YOU WHISPER IT DOESN'T MAKE IT NOT A RAN—

WHAT'S HAPPENING?

I DON'T KNOW, BUT SOMETHING THAT YOU WERE SAYING WAS, LIKE, SUPER CHILL. KEEP TALKING.
MMM HMM. PLEASE CONTINUE SO I CAN RUB MY HANDS TOGETHER AS IF I'M ENJOYING IT.
YOU KNOW, LIKE HOW FLIES DO.

WAIT, YOU GUYS **WANT** ME TO KEEP RANT—
JAMES?!

RANCH! I SAID "RANCH"!
RANCH ON MY ICE CREAM, YUM!
THAT'S **SO MUCH** WORSE THAN PINEAPPLE ON PIZZA.

LET ME TELL YOU HOW I FEEL ABOUT NUTS ON A SUNDAE . . .
I CAN'T BELIEVE I'VE BEEN DOING IT WRONG ALL THIS TIME. I DON'T NEED TO SCREAM FOR PEOPLE TO GET BEHIND WHAT I'M SAYING!
AND HAVING LEARNED THAT, I SUPPOSE YOU'RE GOING TO QUIT WHILE YOU'RE AHEAD?
AAH!
HAHAHAHAHAHA!
AHHHH, CAN YOU IMAGINE?
BUT NO.

BEFORE, NO ONE APPRECIATED MY RANTS.
BUT NOW WITH MY JSMR, JAMES'S SILENT MOUTH RANTS, EVERYONE'S LOVING WHAT I'M SAYING AND LOUDSPEAKER'S NONE THE WISER! SO I'M GONNA **KEEP RANTING.**
GREAT IDEA.

HUH, I WAS MORE EXPECTING AN "I TOLD YOU SO."
EH, I'VE SAID IT TO YOU SO MANY TIMES, IT'S LOST ALL MEANING.
INSTEAD, I'M THINKING THERE'S **GOTTA** BE A WAY TO EXPLOIT THIS.
I MEAN, TAKE ADVANTAGE OF PEOPLE.
I MEAN, MAKE MONEY.

HMM, SHARE MY OPINIONS **AND** MAKE MONEY? I LIKE THE SOUND OF THAT.
ONLY PROBLEM IS THAT YOU HAVE A VERY LIMITED AUDIENCE. ONLY A FEW PEOPLE AT A TIME CAN LEAN IN CLOSE ENOUGH TO HEAR YOUR WHISPERS, AND THAT'S A BAD BUSINESS MODEL.

YEAH, AND I CAN'T INFLUENCE CHANGE IF IT'S ONLY A FEW PEOPLE HEARING ME . . .
BUT I KNOW JUST THE THING TO GET MY WORDS HEARD BY EVERYONE: THE INTERNET!
WHAT'S THE INTERNET?

YOU'RE FROM THE FUTURE! HOW DO YOU NOT KNOW WHAT THE INTERNET IS?!
GUESS IT ISN'T THAT IMPORTANT.

LOOK, THE ONLY **REAL** WAY TO GET YOUR VOICE OUT TO EVERYONE AND MAKE MONEY IS BY SELLING CDS!
ARE YOU **SURE** YOU'RE FROM THE FUTURE?

SOON . . .

. . . BIRTHDAY CAKE ISN'T A PARTY TREAT, IT'S A PARTY CHEAP! THE ONLY REASON WE EAT BIRTHDAY CAKE INSTEAD OF BIRTHDAY PIE IS BECAUSE CAKE CAN BE SLICED MORE WAYS FOR MORE PEOPLE, MAKING IT THE CHEAPER CHOICE. SO WHEN YOU HAVE BIRTHDAY CAKE, IT MEANS YOUR PARTY'S THROWN BY A CHEAPSKATE!

BONK

HOW DO WE LISTEN TO THESE LITTLE FRISBEES?

FOR JUST A **LOT OF DOLLARS** MORE, I'LL SELL YOU A CD PLAYER I GOT FOR FREE AT THE DUMP AND ***YOU'LL*** GET TO ENJOY THEM LIKE ALL THESE GOOD PEOPLE!

NEXT!

I'LL TELL YA, MAX. I WISH SOMEONE HAD TOLD ME TO STOP YELLING SOONER.
I'M PRETTY SURE *EVERYONE'S* TOLD YOU THAT.
I'M JUST SAYING, LOOK AT ALL THE GOOD I'M DOING. JUST BEING MYSELF AND HELPING PEOPLE LEAD HAPPIER LIVES.
MAN, THESE CDS ARE SELLING LIKE *HOT-CAKES.*

WHY ARE *HOTCAKES* THE STANDARD FOR–
SAVE IT FOR THE NEXT CD, BUD.

MAX, MY GLORIOUS VOCAL CORDS FEEL PARCHED.

POP
GACK! ACK!

HACK!!!

MAX! I'M TRYING TO PROTECT MY VOICE SO I CAN RECORD MORE **AND** DO KARAOKE!
I'M SORRY! WITH ALL YOUR WHISPERING, I'VE BEEN ASLEEP SO MUCH MY MUSCLES ARE FATIGUED!

OOH, BLANK CDS ARE HERE. BETTER WARM UP.

GRANNY SMITH APPLES ARE NOT FOR EATING. TART, GREEN, THAT'S A PIE APPLE, PEOPLE! AND DON'T EVEN GET ME STARTED ON RED DELICIOUS—

CLATTER

WHAT'S THIS *JUNK?*
IT'S WHAT THE PEOPLE WANT TO HEAR.

BUT I DON'T HAVE ANYTHING AGAINST SCISSORS.
OTHER THAN BEING TOLD BY MY PARENTS NOT TO RUN WITH THEM.
NO, CUSTOMERS JUST WANT YOU TO *PLAY* WITH THEM, IN FRONT OF THE MICROPHONE.

WAIT. THEY WANT *SOUNDS* INSTEAD OF MY INSPIRED OPINIONS FOR CHANGE?
YOU'VE BEEN SAYING *SENTENCES?*

YES! YOU HAVEN'T BEEN HEARING ME?
WELL, I HAVEN'T BEEN HEARING MUCH. BUT BEFORE I BLACK OUT, I THINK I REMEMBER WHISPERS.

SO NO ONE COULD HEAR ME THIS WHOLE TIME?
IT DOESN'T MATTER, BECAUSE JSMR WORKS!

CLEARLY, IT DOESN'T! PEOPLE HAVEN'T BEEN LISTENING TO ME AT ALL!

I THOUGHT EVERYONE WAS FINALLY EMBRACING MY RANTS, BUT IT'S CLEAR THE ONLY WAY I CAN BE HEARD IS BY RAISING MY VOICE.
BUT YOU CAN'T! YOU'LL BE EXPELLED! AND THAT MEANS NO KARA-POKEY!

IT'S "KARAOKE," MAX.
AND YOU'RE RIGHT. WHICH MEANS I ONLY HAVE ONE CHOICE TO SAVE OUR NIGHT OUT.
YOU'RE GOING TO COME UP WITH A MILLION-DOLLAR IDEA, BUILD YOUR BUSINESS AND SELL IT, AND USE THE MONEY TO BUY THE KARAOKE CLUB SO WE CAN DO KARAOKE ANYTIME WE WANT?

WHAT?! NO. THAT'S WAY TOO MUCH WORK.
I'M GOING TO ...

STOP RANTING.

DO WE NEED TO DO A FLASHBACK OR SOMETHING? TO REMIND YOU OF HOW QUICKLY YOU GAVE IN THE LAST TIME YOU TRIED?
IT'LL BE DIFFERENT THIS TIME. KARAOKE'S TONIGHT, SO I ONLY HAVE TO NOT RANT FOR A FEW HOURS.
AND THIS TIME, I'VE GOT A ***BULLETPROOF PLAN.***

WHAT ARE YOU DOING?
THE FIRST STEP TOWARD NOT RANTING IS CUTTING OFF ALL MY ***SENSES,*** SO I CAN'T BE TRIGGERED.
THANKFULLY, I DON'T HAVE A NOSE.

GLOB GLOB

NOW TO LOD MY-ELF IN DA BAT-ROOM UNDIL IDS LIME.

WHUMP
WELL, AT LEAST WITH HIM NOT ***RANTING,*** I CAN STOP WORRYING ABOUT HIS SAFETY.

. . . SO THEN I LOOK AT THE BIRD IN MY WINDOW AND I'M LIKE, WHAT'S UP? AND YOU KNOW WHAT THE BIRD SAYS TO ME?
TWEET!
AND WE LAUGHED AND WE LAUGHED!
WELL, AT LEAST UNTIL I REALIZED I DON'T SPEAK BIRD.

DE ADD DA KAR-EYE-OKEY GLUB?
UM, YEAH. BUT . . .

YOU GUYS, SOMETHING HORRIBLE HAS HAPPENED!
I'VE GOT ALL THE CASH I FLEECED PEOPLE FOR AND NOWHERE TO SPEND IT!

WIPE WIPE

WAIT, IS *EVERYONE* LISTENING TO JSMR?
JUST BECAUSE YOU QUIT DOING IT DIDN'T MEAN I HAD TO STOP *SELLING* IT.

THAT'S WHY YOU'VE GOT NOWHERE TO SPEND YOUR MONEY.
NOBODY'S DOING ANYTHING BUT BLISSING OUT ON JSMR!

WHICH MEANS . . . !

DIRT'S
KARAOKE CLUB
CLOS

THE KARAOKE CLUB IS *CLOSED!*
HANG ON, JAMES! I'LL GET YOU A RELAXING CHAMOMILE TEA!

TEA HOUSE

TEA PEOPLE SWITCHED TO JSMR, TOO.

I DON'T GET IT. I BE MYSELF AND RANT, I GET IN TROUBLE. I BE A GOOD SOLDIER AND *DON'T* RANT, THE TOWN SHUTS DOWN.
I CAN'T WIN!
WELL, *SOMEONE'S* GOTTA SNAP ALL THESE PEOPLE OUT OF IT SO I CAN GET MY GRUB ON.

HISSSSSS!

AND THAT SOMEONE'S *NOT* GONNA BE ME.
HOW ARE WE GONNA GET THE HOKEY-POKEY CLUB OPEN AGAIN IF THEY WON'T TAKE OFF THEIR HEADPHONES?
"KARAOKE"— AND WE HAVE TO MAKE THEM *WANT* TO TAKE THEM OFF.

AND I KNOW *JUST* HOW TO DO IT.

LOUDSPEAKER SAID HE CAN COME OUT OF ANY SPEAKER—
AND HEAD-PHONES ARE LIKE *LITTLE SPEAKERS!*

BUT WHAT'S HE GONNA SAY TO GET THEM TO TAKE THEM OFF?
HE'S NOT. IT'LL BE
WITH HIS HELP BROADCASTING, THESE JSMRers ARE GOING TO HEAR A RANT COMING THROUGH THEIR EAR SPEAKERS THAT WILL INSPIRE THEM TO TAKE THEM OFF.
SERIOUSLY? DO YOU NEVER LEARN FROM YOUR MISTAKES?
WHAT ARE YOU, NEW?

HELLO, JAMES. GOOD OF YOU TO COME TO SCHOOL, BUT I'M AFRAID THERE IS NO MORE SCHOOL.

BECAUSE THERE'S NO MORE STUDENTS, THANKS TO WHAT I CAN ONLY ASSUME IS A MUCH MORE ENJOYABLE HEADPHONE-BASED LEARNING PROGRAM.
SHUFFLE SHUFFLE

AND WITHOUT STUDENTS TO TEST—
YEAH, ABOUT THAT. THE HEAD-PHONES ARE FOR LISTENING TO JSMR, JAMES'S SILENT MOUTH RANTS.

YOU'VE BEEN *RANTING?!?!*

WAIT, WHY ARE THEY ALL SO HAPPY?
THEY FIND MY WHISPERED VOICE SOOTHING.
SO SOOTHING THAT THEY, AND THE ENTIRE TOWN, WON'T DO ANYTHING WHILE THEY'VE GOT THOSE HEADPHONES ON.

BUT TO GET THEM TO TAKE THE HEADPHONES OFF, I NEED YOU TO GIVE A SECOND CHANCE . . .
. . . TO *RANTS.*

JAMES . . .
JUST HEAR ME OUT! I KNOW IN THE PAST I'VE *SOMETIMES* USED MY RANTS FOR SELFISH REASONS.
ALWAYS.

AND THEY ALWAYS INSPIRE *ACTION,* OFTEN IN THE FORM OF RAGE AND UNREST.
BUT WHAT IF RANTS COULD MAKE PEOPLE WANT TO *LIVE* AGAIN?
TO SHED THEIR HEADPHONES AND RE-EMBRACE WHO THEY ARE, AND MAKE THEM WANT TO SHARE IT WITH THE WORLD?!

. . . AAAAND IF *THAT* DOESN'T WORK, YOU CAN EXPEL ME.
YOU DRIVE A HARD BARGAIN, MISTER!

HELLO, JSMRERS.

I'M HERE TO TELL YOU THAT YOU'VE BEEN LED ASTRAY—BY ME AND JSMR.

JSMR IS NOT THE KEY TO A HAPPY LIFE.
IT'S A SYSTEM THAT HAPPENED BECAUSE I DIDN'T WANT TO GIVE UP RANTING, AND THOUGHT I COULD GET AWAY WITH IT BY WHISPERING.

I MEAN, I TRIED TO STOP SO I WOULDN'T GET EXPELLED, BUT I COULDN'T.
WHY? BECAUSE RANTS ARE WHO I AM AND HOW I COMMUNICATE MY THOUGHTS AND OPINIONS IN HOPES OF INSPIRING CHANGE.

I COULDN'T BE FORCED TO SOME ACCEPTABLE STANDARDIZED VERSION OF MYSELF.
AND NEITHER SHOULD YOU.

THAT'S RIGHT. YOU ARE ALL INDIVIDUALS, EACH AND EVERY ONE OF YOU.
BUT THAT INDIVIDUALITY HAS BEEN TAKEN BY JSMR, WHICH HAS TURNED YOU ALL INTO BLISSFUL ZOMBIES.

IS THAT WHAT YOU WANT TO BE? JUST ANOTHER SMILING ZOMBIE?
OR DO YOU WANT TO BE YOUR TRUE, AUTHENTIC SELF AND SHARE THAT WITH THE WORLD?

IN SUMMARY, IF YOU WANT LASTING HAPPINESS, YOU NEED TO SPEAK OUT AND MAKE CHANGE.
AND YOU CAN'T MAKE CHANGE UNLESS YOU HAVE *VOLUME.*

OH GOOD, HE STOPPED TALKING.

ALL RIGHT, FINE! WE'LL DO THIS THE OLD-SCHOOL WAY: WITH A DIVISIVE OPINION.
DOGS ARE BETTER THAN CATS!

BOOOOO!
YAAAAY!

RELAX, CAT PEOPLE. DOGS ARE ONLY BETTER BECAUSE THEY'RE DUMB ENOUGH TO THINK ANY OWNER IS GREAT.

RAAARGH!
AHAHA HAHA HA!

WHOOOSH

SWSH SWSH

AARRRRGGGHHH!

WELL, AT LEAST I GOT THEM OFF JSMR.
YEAH, AND I GOT BACK ALL THE PLAYERS. THESE THINGS ARE GOING TO BE WORTH BIG BUCKS!
CDS *ARE* THE FUTURE.

SEE, PRINCIPAL LOUDSPEAKER? RANTS CAN DO GOOD.

I'M NOT SURE EVERYONE AGREES, JAMES.

CLANK

INCITING A RIOT OUTSIDE OF SCHOOL IS A SERIOUS CRIME. YOU'RE GOING TO *JAIL!*
JAIL?! BUT— KARAOKE!

MAX, YOU KNOW YOU DIDN'T HAVE TO COME WITH ME TO JAIL.
OH, NOW YOU TELL ME!

HELLO, JAMES, MAX.
SURPRISE!

PRINCIPAL LOUDSPEAKER?
OH, JAMES DIDN'T TELL YOU THAT YOU DON'T NEED TO BE HERE, TOO?

I'M JUST HERE TO THANK YOU, JAMES.
NOW THAT YOU'RE IN JAIL, YOU'RE NOT A STUDENT, SO YOUR TEST SCORES DON'T COUNT. AND SINCE EVERYONE ELSE SHOWED UP WITH THEIR PENCILS AND ACED THEIR STANDARDIZED TESTS, THE SCHOOL IS FULLY FUNDED!

HUH. SO CRIME DOES PAY.
MMHMM. WHICH IS WHY I'M HERE TO REWARD YOU—WITH KARAOKE!

WHAT? WHAT KIND OF LOVE? WOULD PLAY WITH MY HEART?
WHAT? WHAT KIND OF LOVE? WOULD PLAY WITH MY HEART?
AND LEAVE ME ALONE TO DINE OUT?

AWWW, LEAVING YOU NOW. WOULD BREAK MY HEART.
SO HERE I WILL BE, TAMARI SAUCE.
HUH. IT REALLY *IS* "TAMARI SAUCE."
SO HERE I WILL BE, TAMARI SAUCE.
THE END

GERMS
of Endearment
SMIGIEL

HEH HEH
HEH . . .
BREAD.
OH YES.

I SET MY OWN RULES, MY PARENTS HAVE NO IDEA WHAT A REBEL I AM . . . BECAUSE YOU AND I COMMUNICATE IN A SUPER-SECRET FRIEND CODE!

AW, HECK YEAH!
BEAN TIME
70K CALORI

MAN, MY PET'S LAZY. YOU SAID THIS WAS FUN.
IT NEVER MOVES! STUPID NON-PET PET!
SOOP

OKAY. LET ME DECODE THAT.
CODE IS THE FIRST WORD OF EACH SENTENCE:

1. MAN
2. YOU
3. I+
4. STUPID

HEY!
IT WASN'T SUPER-SECRET FRIEND CODE, MAN. MY PET'S JUST LAZY!

NO . . . WAIT, I WAS WRONG. IT'S JUST DEAD.

JIGGLE JIGGLE

MOM'S MEAL. ARRIVING. BE THE BIRD. QUIET.
CAW! CAW!

HI, HONEY. JUST MAKING SURE YOU BRUSHED YOUR TEETH.
GAME OVER MAN
BREAD OH YES.

BLOW INTO THE BRUSHALYZER.

BING
MINTY FRESH

SEE? ALL GOOD.
GUESS YOU CAN LET ME GO BACK TO *NOT* SLEEPING.

YAAAAWWN!
JAMES, I'M A SCIENTIST. I DON'T TRUST TECHNOLOGY.
YANK!

MINTY SMELL, ALL RIGHT . . .
. . . BUT I'M ALSO SEEING *CHOCOLATE CHIP* FRAGMENTS.

CONCLUSION? YOU ATE *MINT CHOCOLATE CHIP ICE CREAM* TO FOOL THE BRUSHALYZER!
WHAAAAT? I DON'T KNOW WHAT YOU'RE TALKING ABOUT!

EITHER YOU DO IT, OR I'LL DO IT.
NO.

JAMES, IT'S *LATE*, PLEASE JUST—
JUST *DO* WHAT YOU *TELL ME?*
THEY'RE *MY* TEETH, AND I SHOULD BE ABLE TO DECIDE WHAT HAPPENS TO THEM!
BREAD OH YES.

WE'VE GONE OVER THIS. UNTIL YOU'RE EIGHTEEN YEARS OF AGE, THEY'RE *MY* TEETH, BECAUSE I'M LEGALLY OBLIGATED TO PAY FOR ALL YOUR DENTAL WORK.

NOW DON'T BE LAZY, *BRUSH!*

PLAQUE PULVERIZER
TEETH! TEETH!
11/10
CAVITY PROTECTION
11 out of 10 dentists recommend!

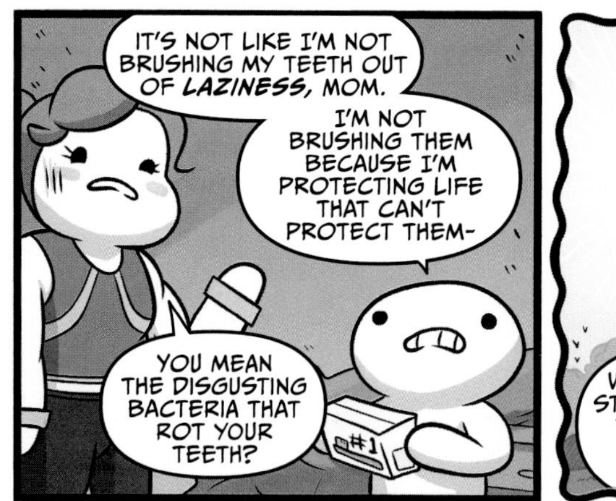

IT'S NOT LIKE I'M NOT BRUSHING MY TEETH OUT OF *LAZINESS,* MOM.
I'M NOT BRUSHING THEM BECAUSE I'M PROTECTING LIFE THAT CAN'T PROTECT THEM-
YOU MEAN THE DISGUSTING BACTERIA THAT ROT YOUR TEETH?
#1

WHY IS IT THAT EVERYONE ONLY WANTS TO PROTECT THE *CUTE* CREATURES?
THE PUPPIES, THE KITTENS, THE KILLER WHALES . . . BUT WHAT ABOUT THE *UGLY* ONES? EVEN *THEY* DESERVE TO LIVE!
WHICH IS WHY I'M MAKING A STAND TO PROTECT THE DISGUSTING BACTERIA IN MY MOUTH.
SURELY YOU CAN'T ASK ME *NOT* TO SAVE LIVES!

I CAN...BUT I WON'T.
OH, COME ON!
WAIT. ***REALLY?***
#1

YES, BECAUSE I'M TIRED. AND NO MATTER HOW MANY TIMES I TELL YOU NOT TO METAPHORICALLY STICK A FORK IN A SOCKET, YOU'RE GOING TO DO IT.
SO YOU'LL JUST HAVE TO LEARN THIS LESSON ON YOUR OWN AS WELL.

CHALLENGE ACCEPTED! AND WHEN NOTHING BAD HAPPENS TO ME AND I PROVE I CAN MAKE MY OWN DECISIONS WITHOUT CONSEQUENCE, YOU HAVE TO AGREE TO *NEVER* TELL ME WHAT TO DO WITH MY BODY EVER AGAIN!
OKAY, HONEY. WHEN THAT DOESN'T WORK OUT, I *ALSO* WON'T TELL YOU WHAT YOUR PUNISHMENT IS . . . BECAUSE AS ALWAYS, YOU'LL HAVE ALREADY PUNISHED YOURSELF.

YOU AREN'T BRUSHING YOUR *TEETH?!* BUT THAT CAN HAVE *DIRE* ***CONSEQUENCES!!!***

YOU HEARD ALL OF THAT?
YEAH, YOU FORGOT TO PUT YOUR CAN ON MUTE.

MUTE

BREAD. OH YES.
I DON'T KNOW WHAT YOUR PROBLEM IS WITH BRUSHING. IT'S FUN!
YOU GET TO SEE OLD FRIENDS, HANG OUT, WATCH THEM HAVE A BITE, AND YOUR TEETH GET CLEAN! THEY EVEN RIP OUT THE WORN ONES WHEN IT'S TIME FOR A REPLACEMENT!

WHAT IN THE WORLD ARE YOU TALKING ABOUT?
WATCH!

IT'S CLEANING TIME!

RAT-
A-TAT-
A-TAT-A-TAT
SHING

GUESS IT WAS TIME FOR A REPLACEMENT!

HNNGH!

POP

YEAH, PRETTY SURE I CAN'T REGROW TEETH.
AND I'M GOING TO STICK TO MY GUNS ON NOT BRUSHING AND SHOW MY MOM I CAN MAKE MY OWN DECISIONS WITHOUT CONSEQUENCE.
BUT AS LONG AS I'VE KNOWN YOU, YOU ALWAYS FAIL MISERABLY . . .

WAIT, DID ONE OF YOUR CRAZY RANTS WORK OUT *BEFORE* I MET YOU?!
THEY'VE *ALL* WORKED OUT IN MY SELECTIVE MEMORY, MAX.
BESIDES, HOW CAN I *NOT* DO THIS? IT'LL SAVE LIVES!

OH, COME ON. YOU DON'T REALLY BELIEVE THAT, DO YOU?
I BELIEVE WHATEVER JUSTIFIES MY ACTIONS AND MAKES ME LOOK GOOD TO MYSELF.

HUH. I NEVER THOUGHT OF IT THAT WAY!

THANK YOU FOR YOUR SACRIFICE.

AAAH!

SUP?

GAH! WHAT ARE YOU DOING IN MY MOUTH?!
HEY, DON'T GET UPSET WITH ME. YOU LAID OUT THE RED CARPET BY REFUSING TO BRUSH.

AND NOW I'M HOME . . .

AND I AIN'T GOIN' NOWHERE!

YES!
CONK!
OW!
WHY WOULD I DO THAT?
NORMALLY PEOPLE MEET MY KIND AND BREAK OUT THE TOOTH-PASTE.
"YOU'RE GOING TO HELP ME SHOW MY MOM THAT GOOD *CAN* COME FROM MY DECISIONS!"
GOOD MORNING! TODAY MIGHT POSSIBLY BE THE BEST DAY OF MY LIFE!
JAMES, I, TOO, USED TO NOT BRUSH MY TEETH, BUT THEN I MET YOUR MOTHER . . .
MOUTH WASH
FRESH
THE NEWS
HAM?

SAVE YOUR HORROR STORY, DAD.
I'VE MADE MY DECISION, AND NOT BRUSHING IS ALREADY HAVING POSITIVE RESULTS!

WAUGH!
THAT'S NICE, HONEY.
THE NE

UH, LOUISE? YOU MIGHT WANT TO LOOK AT THIS.
IS IT JAMES SUFFERING THE CONSEQUENCES OF HIS ACTIONS?
NO. I'M NOT, MOM. EVERYTHING'S FINE.

I DUNNO ABOUT "FINE." I MEAN, THERE'S A *LIVING THING* IN YOUR MOUTH . . .
PATRICK, JUST LET HIM LEARN HIS LESSON THE HARD WAY.
MOUTH WASH

OKAY, BUT ISN'T THAT CHILD ENDANGERMENT?
I MEAN, I KNOW I'M NORMALLY THE ***COOL DAD,*** BUT I DON'T THINK I'D DO SO WELL IN PRISON IF SOMEBODY BROUGHT CHARGES.

JAMES, PLEASE GARGLE THIS MOUTHWASH.
SORRY, DAD. BUT NO.

COME ON. HOW ABOUT IF I MAKE IT FUN AND PUT IT IN THIS SUPER SOAKER?
MOUTH WASH

NEW
PSSHHHH
YEAH, THAT ISN'T FUN.

SAFETY FELLA!
BE COOL MAN

I'M TELLING YOU, MAX. WE'VE BEEN LIED TO FOR YEARS BY BIG TOOTH-PASTE!
BIG TOOTHPASTE? SOUNDS LIKE A CRAZY CONSPIRACY THEORY THAT CAN'T POSSIBLY BE TRUE.

TELL ME *MORE!*
I WOULDN'T DO IT JUSTICE. I'LL LET MY NEW PAL TELL YOU.
MEET MAX 2!

WHASSUP, CROCADILLIO?

AWW, YOU NAMED HIM AFTER ME?
WELL, YEAH.

YOU'RE MY OLDEST BEST FRIEND AND HE'S MY NEWEST BEST FRIEND.
BEST FRIEND?! BUT YOU JUST MET HIM!

HAHA! MAX GOT REPLACED BY A STINKING LUMP OF MOUTH GERMS!

YOUR PERSONAL ATTACKS WILL NEVER FILL THE VOID LEFT IN YOU BY YOUR INSECURITY OF NOT HAVING BONES.

HAHAHAHAHAHA!
WHADDAYA TALKING ABOUT? LOOK! I'VE GOT BONES!
SHGLURP
FIZZLE
AHAHAHAHAHAHA!
SEE, MAX? NO NEED TO FEEL THREATENED.
MAX 2'S JUST BETTER THAN YOU AT MAKING ME LOOK GOOD. THAT'S HOW I KNOW HE'S A *GOOD* BACTERIA!
WELL . . . ALL RIGHT.
BUT I'M STILL NOT SURE I LIKE HIM HAVING "BEST FRIEND" NEXT TO HIS NAME.

WHY YOU STARING DAGGERS AT ME LIKE THAT?
OH, SORRY. THAT WAS FOR MAX 2, BUT YOUR MOUTH WAS CLOSED.

YOU WANT ME TO OPEN IT?
NAH, THE MOMENT'S PASSED. I'LL JUST GO ALONG WITH YOUR CRAZY IDEAS UNTIL IT BECOMES CLEAR YOU'RE IN TROUBLE.

LATER . . .

BET YOUR *OTHER* BEST FRIEND CAN'T REACH THIS!

FLICK

MATH IS
RADICAL!
AND HOW!
1+1=FUN!

LATER STILL . . .

WHIPAH!

SNAP

PIZZA DAY

AW, I WANTED PIZZA.

BUUUURRP

THUD THUD THUD THUD

UM . . .

OOF . . .
PHEW . . .

WHY'RE YOU GASSY? YOU DIDN'T EAT THE PIZZA.
NO, UM, IT'S JUST . .

I'M NOT SURE MAX 2 IS A GOOD BACTERIA.
WHAT GAVE YOU THAT IDEA?

WELL, YOUR BREATH STINKS SO MUCH YOU MADE PEOPLE HAVE TO TAKE A NAP.
AT LEAST I ***HOPE*** THEY WERE NAPPING.

WHAT'RE YOU, JEALOUS? THAT'S MY ***NATURAL MUSK!***

YEAH, DON'T HATE ON MAX 2. IT'S NOT LIKE THEY MAKE DEODORANT FOR YOUR MOUTH.
UM, I'M PRETTY SURE THEY DO.

MAX, YOU CAN'T EAT DEODORANT.
I'M TALKING ABOUT *TOOTHPASTE,* MAN!

GASP!
BUT THAT HAS *FLUORIDE!* YOU CAN'T REALLY WANT TO *HURT* MAX 2?!

'COURSE HE DOES.
HE'S TRYING TO GET RID OF ME!

BECAUSE YOU'RE A BAD INFLUENCE!
YOU WANT TO DESTROY INNOCENT LIFE, BUT *I'M* THE BAD INFLUENCE?

GIMME MY *NAME* BACK!
PLEASE, I'M MORE DESERVING OF THE NAME THAN *YOU!*

BWAAAAHHHAHA!
IT HURTS 'CUZ IT MAY BE TRUE!

OKAY, OKAY. EVERYONE CHILL.
MAX 2, MAX IS MY FRIEND AND WOULD NEVER DO *ANYTHING* TO HURT ME.

AND MAX, MAX 2 IS *ALSO* MY FRIEND AND WOULD NEVER DO ANYTHING TO HURT *ME.*

RIGHT, MAX 2?
RIGHT.

BUT I'LL EAT YOUR BABIES, MAX.

OKAY, THAT'S MAKING ME THINK YOU HAVE SOME *BAD* IN YOU TOO.
BUT AS LONG AS YOU DON'T HARM ME IN ANY WAY, I'LL JUST TELL MYSELF YOU WERE JOKING.

CRUNCH

OW!

OH, SORRY. I DIDN'T MEAN TO WAKE YOU.
I WAS JUST HAVING BREAKFAST.

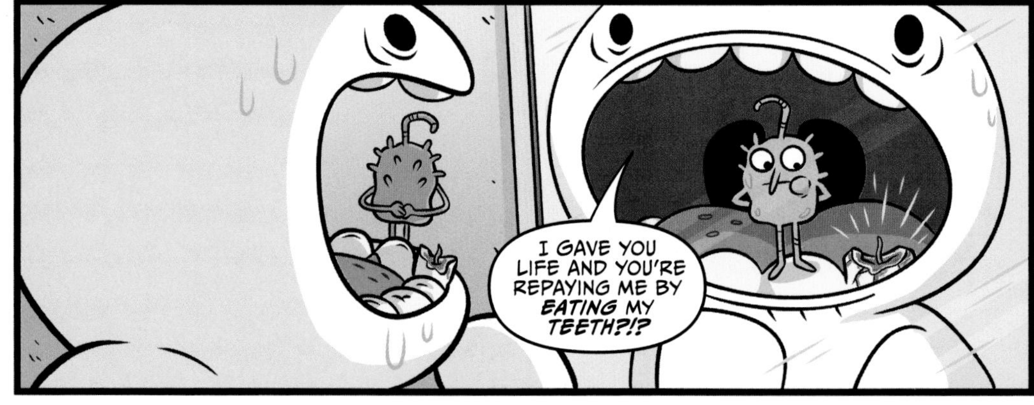
I GAVE YOU LIFE AND YOU'RE REPAYING ME BY *EATING* MY *TEETH?!?*

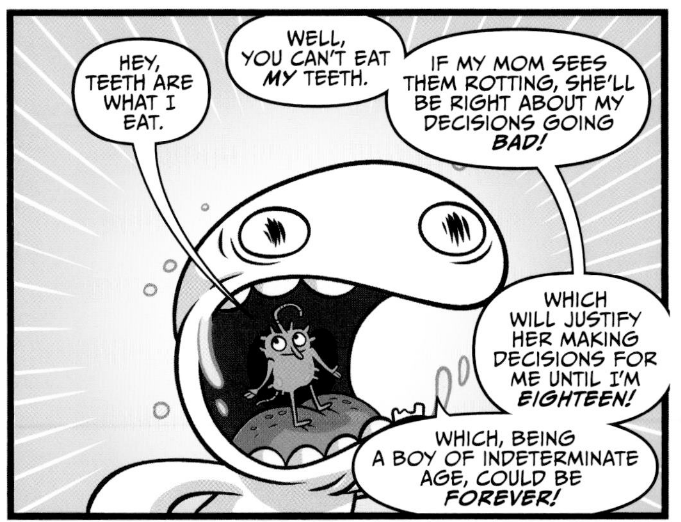

HEY, TEETH ARE WHAT I EAT.
WELL, YOU CAN'T EAT *MY* TEETH.
IF MY MOM SEES THEM ROTTING, SHE'LL BE RIGHT ABOUT MY DECISIONS GOING *BAD!*
WHICH WILL JUSTIFY HER MAKING DECISIONS FOR ME UNTIL I'M *EIGHTEEN!*
WHICH, BEING A BOY OF INDETERMINATE AGE, COULD BE *FOREVER!*

WELL I GOTTA EAT, OR YOU AIN'T SAVING *ANYONE,* AND THEN SHE CAN CALL YOUR BLUFF!

HMM. YOU'RE RIGHT.
HEY, WHAT IF I CAN GET YOU OTHER PEOPLE'S TEETH?

I'M GOOD WITH TAKEOUT.

T.H.

I DON'T LIKE HELPING YOU WITH THIS. I MEAN, YOU SURE THE TUTUS ARE NECESSARY?
YES! WE HAVE TO LOOK LIKE THE TOOTH FAIRY IN CASE ANY OF THESE LITTLE KIDS WAKE UP. DON'T WANNA FREAK THEM OUT OR ANYTHING.

WAIT, WHAT DO WE SAY IF THE TOOTH FAIRY CATCHES *US?*
WE DON'T HAVE WINGS! SHE'LL KNOW!

OH YEAH, *THAT'S* THE STUFF!

NNN . . .

FOODBALL
JOE'S

FOODBA
JOE'S

WAS THAT AN EXPIRED COUPON?
WELL, IT'S BETTER THAN WHAT THE *NEXT* KID'S GETTING.

LINT?
KIND OF. BUT THERE'S A CANDY CENTER.

I'M STILL HUNNNNGRY!

COME ON, MAX. SOUNDS LIKE WE'VE GOT A LOT MORE TEETH TO STEAL.

CRASH

TOLD YOU WE NEEDED WINGS!

WELL, THAT WAS CREEPY.

OH COME ON, WE JUST DID WHAT KIDS THINK THE TOOTH FAIRY DOES: SNEAKS INTO THEIR ROOMS AND STEALS THEIR BABY TEETH TO FEED A SENTIENT MOUTH BACTERIA.
THERE'S NOTHING CREEPY ABOUT THAT.

BOUUURRP

OKAY, PARTNERS. WHERE TO NEXT?

WHAT?! WE JUST SPENT ALL NIGHT GETTING YOU TEETH!
YEAH, BABY TEETH. YOU WANT ME NOT TO DIE, I NEED SOMETHING MORE SUBSTANTIAL.
LIKE ADULT TEETH. OR, AT A MINIMUM, TWEEN TEETH.

HOW ARE WE SUPPOSED TO GET THOSE? BABY TEETH FALL OUT, TWEEN AND ADULT TEETH DON'T.
SOME DO. WHEN THEY HAVE AN ACCIDENT.

OH, WELL, I GUESS IF IT'S AN ACCIDENT.
YEAH. AN ACCIDENT YOU **HELP** WITH.

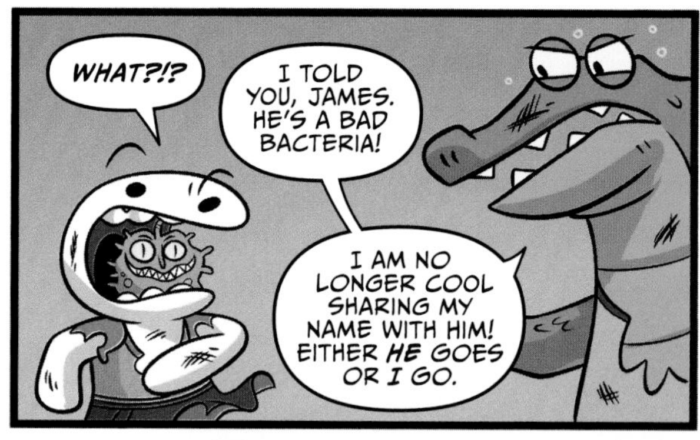
WHAT?!?
I TOLD YOU, JAMES. HE'S A BAD BACTERIA!
I AM NO LONGER COOL SHARING MY NAME WITH HIM! EITHER ***HE*** GOES OR ***I*** GO.

BUT GETTING RID OF HIM WOULD MEAN ADMITTING TO MY MOM THAT SOMETHING BAD HAPPENED FROM MY DECISION TO STOP BRUSHING!
WELL, THEN YOU'LL BE HELPING PEOPLE LOSE THEIR TEETH WITHOUT ***ME!***
THE CROCODILE FORMERLY KNOWN AS MAX!

GO DIRT HIGH!
GO!

WHAT THE HECK ARE WE DOING HERE?
GETTING YOU MORE TEETH.

TODAY IS DODGEBALL, AND THE LAST TIME WE PLAYED, STUART KNOCKED OUT SOMEONE'S TEETH.
SMART. TOLD YOU ACCIDENTS WERE THE WAY TO GO.

SCORE
FOR JAMES. I DO HAVE BONES

OR NOT.

HEY! I *LIKED* YOUR VIOLENT PLAN!
SO DID I, BEFORE I REALIZED STUART'S STILL MAD AT ME FOR YOU EMBARRASSING HIM!

NEED I REMIND YOU OF THE STAKES HERE?
PRETTY SURE WE'VE SAID IT LIKE TEN TIMES THIS EPISODE, SO YES I *KNOW!*
IF I LOSE MY TEETH, MY MOM WILL *STILL* USE IT AGAINST ME!

HOW? YOU'RE LOSING TEETH IN *GYM CLASS,* NOT BECAUSE YOU DIDN'T *BRUSH.* IT'S ALL GOOD!
MAN, YOU'RE EVEN BETTER AT JUSTIFYING IRRESPONSIBLE BEHAVIOR THAN I AM.

FWEEET

YAAAAAHHH!!!

AFTER SCHOOL . . .

I HOPE YOU'RE SATISFIED. NOW I'M MISSING A TOOTH.
SATISFIED UNTIL DINNER.

WHAT? I'M A GROWING GERM!

SO YOU BETTER KEEP PROVIDING. OR ELSE!

BUT I CAN'T GIVE YOU MORE OF MINE.
IT'S NOT LIKE I CAN GROW TEETH LIKE MAX.

WAIT. THAT'S IT! I KNOW HOW TO GET YOU MORE TEETH THAN YOU COULD EVER NEED AND WITHOUT ANY CONSEQUENCES FOR MYSELF!

BUUUUT YOU'LL HAVE TO LIVE IN MAX'S MOUTH NOW.
WHOA, HO HO! NOW WE'RE TALKIN'!
HOW YOU GONNA GET HIM ON BOARD?

WE'LL HAVE TO SNEAK YOU IN.
YOU'RE GONNA BETRAY YOUR FRIEND LIKE THAT?
MAN, YOU REALLY DO WANT TO PROVE YOUR MOM WRONG.

WE'VE GOT A HISTORY.

OKAY, FIRST I GOTTA GET MAX ON OUR SIDE. BETTER PRACTICE WHAT I'M GOING TO SAY TO HIM.

MAX, PLEASE DON'T BE MAD. MAX 2 A FRIEND. IS LIKE YOU. BAD HE'S NOT. INFLUENCE YOU CAN'T. GET HIM TO SEPARATE FROM. ME, SO STOP SAYING THAT I NEED. TOOTHPASTE, AND LET'S BE FRIENDS!
BREAD. OH YES.

NO WONDER YOU NEEDED MY HELP ON THAT TEST, YOUR GRAMMAR'S HORRIBLE!

ALL RIGHT, NOW JUST KEEP QUIET UNTIL I CAN GET YOU INTO HIS MOUTH.

I WANT TO APOLOGIZE TO YOU, WITH NO ULTERIOR MOTIVES. I'M SORRY I LISTENED TO MAX 2 AND MADE YOU FEEL SECOND BEST.

AWW, THANKS! I MISSED YOU!

SQUEAK

OH HEY, IS THAT YOUR SODA? DO YOU MIND IF I TAKE A SIP, THEN *YOU* IMMEDIATELY TAKE A SIP AFTERWARD?
SURE, BUT FIRST YOU NEED TO TRY THE CAKE!
HEFTY GULP

OPEN WIDE!

THAT AIN'T APOLOGY CAKE! THE FROSTING'S MADE OF PLAQUE PULVERIZER TOOTHPASTE!
HE WAS GONNA KILL ME!

MAX! HOW *COULD* YOU?!
YOU ASKED ME TO!
WAIT, DID I GET THE CODE WRONG AGAIN?

FOR YOUR PATHETIC ATTEMPT AT STOPPING ME . . .
I'M GOING TO EAT ALL YOUR TEETH, BUBBLE BOY!

SLAP

CHOMP!

YUM! GROSS!

HEFTY GULP

EW!
WHAT THE
HECK?!

WHOA,
HO HO!
YOU
JUST SENT
ME TO TOOTH
HEAVEN!

NOPE. I SENT
YOU TO H-E-
DOUBLE-HOCKEY-
STICKS.

MAX! IT'S
CLEANING
TIME!

HEY! OW!
STOP! OW!

AAAND, I'M
DEAD.

PHEW! SORRY ABOUT THAT, MAX. I DIDN'T KNOW WHAT ELSE TO DO.
FRIENDS?

FRIENDS. JUST DON'T EVER SPIT IN MY MOUTH AGAIN.
SQUAWK!!

RAT -A- TAT-A- TAT

HI, MOM.
JAMES, WHAT ARE YOU DOING?

I'M STILL NOT BRUSHING, *THAT'S* WHAT I'M DOING.

JUST BECAUSE IT HAS WINGS, JAMES, DOESN'T MEAN IT'S *NOT* A TOOTHBRUSH. THANK YOU FOR BRUSHING YOUR TEETH.
GROOAAANNNN. . .
THE END

BIRTHDAY BAGGERS

YOU THINK MAZ SCARE-AH'S GONNA LIKE OUR BIRTHDAY GIFT?
THE BETTER QUESTION IS, WILL *WE* LOVE HER PARTY'S GOODIE BAGS?
I WILL IF THEY'RE FILLED WITH FUN OR FUN-RELATED ITEMS!
I BET THEY'LL BE PACKED WITH GIFT CARDS . . . OR PACKS OF MAGIC: THE ASSEMBLY CARDS.
OOO, OR MAGIC: THE ASSEMBLY CARDS GIFT CARDS!

I BET THE GOODIE BAGS WILL BE FILLED WITH *CAKE!*
CAKE? WHY WOULD YOU WANT MORE CAKE? THERE'S ALREADY CAKE AT THE PARTY.

BUT IT'S IN A *BAG!*

NEANDER, ROCKING THAT UNIBROW. LIKE A BOSS!
STUART, NO BULLYING. PARTY TIME'S PEACE TIME, AM I RIGHT?

HEY, THANKS FOR HAVING US.
PARTY FAVORS AREN'T OUT YET, HUH? OOO, ARE THEY A *SURPRISE?*
I'VE HEARD OF SURPRISE PARTIES, BUT SURPRISE PARTY *FAVORS?*
MWAH!

OH, UM.
SURPRISE.
THERE AREN'T ANY PARTY FAVORS.

NO PARTY FAVORS?!?!

WAIT, WHAT ABOUT GOODIE BAGS?
THEY'RE THE SAME THING.
AND THEY'RE FOR BABIES.

BABIES? *BABIES?!* WELL, AT LEAST BABIES HONOR SOCIAL CONTRACTS!
WHAT? WHEN HAS A BABY EVER HONORED ANYTHING?

EVERYONE KNOWS A GIFT FOR A GOODIE BAG IS THE UNSPOKEN AGREEMENT—
BUT HOW DOES EVERYONE KNOW IF IT'S UNSPOKEN?

THEY JUST—
I DON'T KNOW! BUT THE POINT IS, THEY *DO*, AND IT'S AN AGREEMENT AS OLD AS TIME.
YOU BRING A GIFT TO A BIRTHDAY PARTY, YOU GET SOMETHING IN RETURN!
THERE'S CAKE. WE COULD JUST PUT SOME OF THE CAKE IN A BAG . . .

CAKE IN A BAG IS NOT A PARTY FAVOR, MAX!
COOL. WELL, I'M GONNA PUT ON MUSIC SO WE CAN ALL STAND AROUND AWKWARDLY AND NOT DANCE WITH EACH OTHER.

COME ON, MAX. WE'RE GOING TO TAKE OUR GIFT AND GIVE IT TO SOMEONE WHO HONORS THE AGREEMENT!

A PARTY WHERE YOU BRING SOMETHING AND GET NOTHING IN RETURN? WHAT HAS THE WORLD COME TO, MAX?
BUT AREN'T BIRTHDAY PARTIES ABOUT THE PERSON WHOSE BIRTHDAY IT IS, AND NOT ABOUT, YOU KNOW . . .
. . . YOU?
THIS IS WHY WE'RE FRIENDS, MAX.
SO I CAN TALK SENSE INTO YOU?
HA HA. NO.
SO I CAN SHOW YOU HOW TO TURN LEMONS INTO LEMONADE.
WELL, I GUESS A BEVERAGE WOULD BE GOOD. THIS BAG CAKE'S A LITTLE DRY.
I BET THERE ARE PARTY FAVORS AT *THIS* PARTY.

WELL, SINCE WE WEREN'T INVITED, THERE'S NO WAY TO FIND OUT. COME ON, LET'S GET SOME LEMONADE.
NO, MAX.

WE'RE GOING IN.

DID YOU NOT HEAR WHAT I JUST SAID?
MAN, I FEEL LIKE I'M TALKING TO MYSELF SOMETIMES.

KIDS THIS AGE **HAVE** TO INVITE EVERYONE. WE'LL JUST BLEND IN, DELIVER MAZ'S GIFT, AND LEAVE WITH A GOODIE BAG.

BUT TO BLEND IN WE'LL HAVE TO MAKE OURSELVES LOOK **YOUNGER.**

MAN, I FORGOT BEING YOUNGER WAS SO PAINFUL.

BOUNCY HOUSE!
BE COOL, MAX. BE COOL!

WHO ARE YOU?
WE'RE, UH, ROBBY AND JORDAN, YOUR TWIN COUSINS.

THAT PRESENT FOR ME?

LEAST WE COULD DO TO FULFILL OUR PART OF THE GIFT FOR GOODIE BAG AGREEMENT.

UNICORN HORN POLISH?
THIS MUST MEAN MY PARENTS ARE GETTING ME A *UNICORN!*
MOM! DAD!
SEE, MAX? THAT'S HOW IT'S SUPPOSED TO WORK. NOW COME ON. GRAB A GOODIE BAG.

BOUNCY HOUSE!!!!
ALL RIGHT, YOU ENJOY. I'LL SEE WHAT THESE BAGS OF GOODNESS ARE ALL ABOUT.

WHY WOULD ANYONE EVER WANT TO GROW OUT OF *THIS?*
DAZED AND CONE-FUSED GIFT CARD
J.FO

AM I *RIGHT*, DECLAN?

BOUNCY CAKE! BOUNCY CAKE!

PSSSSSSSHH

AAAAAA!!!
PSSSSSSHHHHHHH

OOO BOY. YEAH. THAT'S NOT GOOD.

MUST BE A FACTORY DEFECT.
THAT WE HAD NOTHING TO DO WITH.

AHAHAHAHAHAHAHA!

WHAT'RE YOU CHUCKLEHEADS LAUGHING ABOUT?
AND WHERE'D YOU GET ALL THE COOL STUFF?!
DAZED AND

WE CRASHED A KID'S PARTY AND GOT US SOME PARTY FAVORS.
OO! OO! I WANT IN! I LOVE ILL-GOTTEN GAINS!
SPLAT

HEE HEE HEE HEE!
MINUS THOSE STICKY HANDS. THEY WORK, LIKE, ONCE, THEN DON'T STICK TO ANYTHING.

SPLAT

THIS THING SUCKS!

ECHO, YOUR WONT FOR PARTICIPATING IN BORDERLINE LAWLESS ACTIVITIES GIVES ME AN IDEA.
WE CAN KEEP THIS GOING.
YES! FREE STUFF AT SOMEONE ELSE'S EXPENSE!

ALL WE NEED TO DO IS SPOT MAILBOXES WITH BALLOONS TIED TO THEM AND IT'S PARTY-CRASHING TIME!
YOU'RE GONNA BUY PRESENTS FOR KIDS YOU DON'T EVEN KNOW?

YOU'RE RIGHT. WE CAN'T VIOLATE THE SACRED UNSPOKEN AGREEMENT.
THE GIFT FOR GOODIE BAG AGREEMENT SAYS YOU HAVE TO BRING A GIFT . . .

. . . BUT IT DOESN'T SAY IT HAS TO BE A GOOD GIFT!
WE CAN GET CHEAP KNOCKOFFS FOR GIFTS AT THE 89-CENT STORE.
SO YOU'RE GOING TO WORK THE PARTY SYSTEM, IN YOUR FAVOR, ON OTHER KIDS' BIRTHDAYS?

I'M OKAY WITH THAT.
IT'S NOT THAT BAD. KIDS DON'T PAY FOR PARTY FAVORS, PARENTS DO. PLUS, THEY'LL GET AN EXTRA GIFT.
BUT WON'T CRUMMY GIFTS MAKE KIDS ANGRY?

POSSIBLY, BUT *WE'LL* NEVER KNOW, BECAUSE WE'LL DUCK OUT BEFORE GIFTS ARE OPENED, AND GRAB A GOODIE BAG FROM THE TABLE ON THE WAY.
MAN, IT'S GOOD YOU DON'T USE YOUR BRAIN FOR *REAL* EVIL.

LATER . . .
89¢
STORE

89¢
BUNDAM
DO NOT PLAY WITH IN NON VENTILATED AREA

89¢
SPRING UNDER TENSION CATAPULT RISK
SLANKY

SO STICKY IT'LL TAKE A SURGEON TO REMOVE IT
89 CENTS

NOT FOR USE BY OPEN FLAME

WE'RE YOUR NEW NEIGHBORS, JIM, JOHN, AND JOANIE. JUST MOVED TO THE BIG CITY FROM COW COUNTRY, YA HEAR?

MOO!

WE'RE YOUR NEW CLASSMATES: GEORGE, ALSO GEORGE, AND ALSO GEORGE ASWELL.

OUR PARENTS WERE LAZY.

HI, WE'RE YOUR COUSINS: APPLE, ORANGE, AND BANANA.

I CAN SEE THE FAMILY RESEMBLANCE.

ZUPE
GOODIES VS GIFTS
GOOOODIES
GIFTS

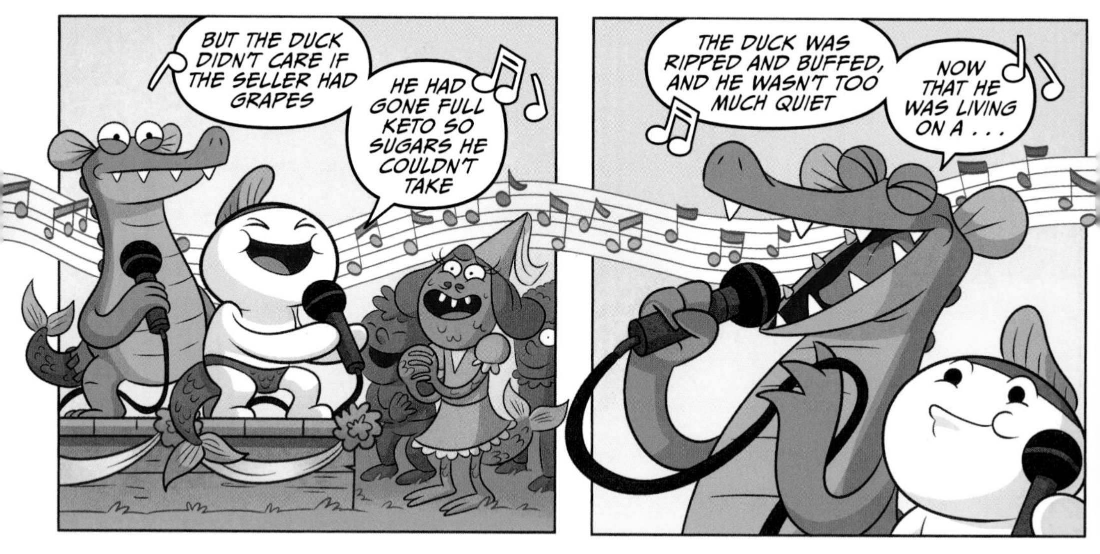
BUT THE DUCK DIDN'T CARE IF THE SELLER HAD GRAPES
HE HAD GONE FULL KETO SO SUGARS HE COULDN'T TAKE
THE DUCK WAS RIPPED AND BUFFED, AND HE WASN'T TOO MUCH QUIET
NOW THAT HE WAS LIVING ON A . . .

HIGH-FAT DIET!!!

YEAH!
WOOOO!
ENCORE!

HUH, THIS ONE'S REALLY LIGHT.

BETTER OPEN IT FIRST SO IT DOESN'T GET CRUSHED.

GO

TIME TO GO!

COTTON BALLS?!?

WHY DIDN'T YOU TELL US IT WAS TIME TO GO?!

IS THIS A *JOKE?*
WHO BROUGHT ME A ***COTTON BALL ASSORTMENT*** AS A GIFT?
I SWEAR, I WILL SEND YOU TO THE ***BOTTOM OF THE SEA!***

IT WAS *YOU!*

WHAT? NO. I MEAN, COME ON, JUST 'CUZ WE'RE SNEAKING OUT?

LOOK, IF IT WERE US WE'D TELL YOU, BECAUSE THAT'S A PRETTY SWEET GIFT.
SOOOOO MANY USES FOR COTTON BALLS.

LIKE WHAT?
UM . . . APPLYING CALAMINE LOTION!
AND, UH . . . DRESSING UP LIKE GEORGE WASHINGTON!
WHITE HAIR . . . HEH HEH.

SOMEONE GAVE ME A CASE OF COTTON SWABS AT MY BIRTHDAY LAST WEEK.

JIM, JOSH, AND JANEY WERE THERE TOO! BUT WITH NO TAILS.
AT MY PARTY THEY TOLD ME THEIR NAMES WERE BOB, BRAD, AND BARBIE!
WHY DO THEY HAVE SUCH STUPID AND ALLITERATED NAMES?

TIME TO GO!
OH, NOW YOU SAY IT!

LOOK! A DISTRACTION!

WELL, IT WAS FUN WHILE IT LASTED.
WHOA, WHOA, WHOA, WHOA. WHY ARE YOU TALKING ABOUT STOPPING?
WE JUST GOT OVERCONFIDENT AND WEREN'T KEEPING TRACK OF TIME.
I TOLD YOU THIS WAS GOING TO COME BACK TO HAUNT YOU.

NO, YOU DIDN'T. YOU JUST THOUGHT IT WAS BAD FORM.
IT'S THE SAME THING! AND NOW YOU'LL BE HAUNTED BY *GHOSTS!*

WE'RE REALLY GIVING UP ON THIS? BUT THAT MEANS I HAVE TO GROW UP AND ACCEPT A LIFE EVENT I DON'T PARTICULARLY CARE FOR.
. . . WHICH I'M SURE YOU'LL HANDLE WITH GRACE.

AHAHAHAHAHAHAHA!

AHH, WE HAVE FUN, DON'T WE?

89¢
SPRING UNDER TENSION CATAPULT RISK

HEY, MAX. SIT ON THIS!
OKAY.
SLANKY

ZWIP

SPROING

WELL, AT LEAST THESE LEFTOVER GIFTS ARE GOOD FOR *SOMETHING.*
SLANKY

YOU GOTTA SEE THIS— WHERE'S MAX?

SMASHHHH!!
THERE HE IS!

DO IT AGAIN!
I GUESS WE **COULD** USE A THIRD SKYLIGHT.
WAIT, WAIT, WAIT, WAIT, WAIT.

BEFORE YOU DO MORE SENSELESS RENOVATIONS—
SENSELESS? LOOK HOW MUCH MORE NATURAL LIGHT MAX LET IN.

WILL YOU JUST LET ME TELL YOU WHAT I CAME UP HERE TO TELL YOU, WHICH IN MY HEAD I IMAGINED YOU TWO GETTING REALLY EXCITED ABOUT?!?

THANK YOU.

THIS PARTY INVITE JUST MYSTERIOUSLY BLEW IN MY WINDOW!
NOT INTERESTED. NOW, CAN I CREATE SOME MORE SUN HOLES?

NO. BECAUSE THIS INVITE IS ALMOST TOO GOOD TO BE TRUE!
THEY'RE OFFERING AN INSANE PARTY FAVOR: A NEW XBLOCKS WITH ALL THE GAMES, WORTH A THOUSAND DOLLARS!
WOW!

IS THAT A LOT OF MONEY?
WAIT. THEY PUT THE PARTY FAVOR VALUE *ON* THE INVITE?

YES, AND I'M SURE WE SHOULD READ MORE INTO THAT, BUT I'M TOO EXCITED ABOUT THE PLAN I HAVE TO GET IN AND GET OUT WITHOUT US GETTING CAUGHT.

YOU JUST HAVE THAT WAITING?

YOU HAVE A LOT OF PLANS.

FIRST, BY NOW EVERYONE HAS HEARD ABOUT US ON THE PARTY CIRCUIT, SO WE'LL NEED FRESH CHARACTERS.
CLICK

MAX, YOUR NEW CHARACTER IS RANDALL, A DISTANT COUSIN FROM THE MIDWEST WHO DRIVES A BIG RIG TO SUPPORT HIS SEQUINED-VEST COLLECTING HABIT.
YOU'LL NEED TO MAKE YOUR TAIL A PONYTAIL.
CLICK

I'D HAVE PREFERRED A MULLET, BUT *FINE.*

ECHO, YOU'RE GONNA PLAY PRECOCIOUS: A KID SCIENTIST WHO JUST MOVED FROM ANTARCTICA AND CAN'T STOP CORRECTING PEOPLE ABOUT PENGUINS NOT EXISTING AT THE NORTH POLE.

SO . . . UNBELIEVABLE, AND ANNOYING.
AND YOU'LL NEED TO TAKE OFF YOUR BOOTS AND WALK, OR THEY'LL REALIZE WHO YOU REALLY ARE.

FINE, I'LL TAKE OFF THE BOOTS, BUT I'M NOT WALKING.

WHAT? THEY'RE NOT BOOTS!

AND SECOND, WE KNOW THE PAYOFF IS BIG, SO WE CAN ACTUALLY BRING A LEGIT GOOD GIFT THAT WON'T GET US CHASED OUT IF IT'S OPENED BEFORE THE GOODIE BAGS ARE BROUGHT OUT.
HUH, OTHER THAN THE RIDICULOUS ROLES, YOU'VE ACTUALLY GOT A PRETTY SOLID PLAN FOR ONCE.
LEGIT GOOD GIFT

WEIRD, RIGHT? OKAY, HANDS IN ON THREE!

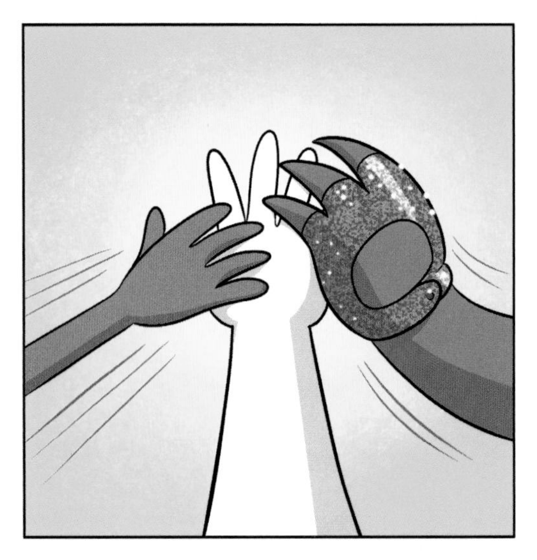

WHAT? IF RANDALL'S DRIVING TRUCKS, HE DON'T WANT CALLUSES!

SOON . . .
WAIT A MINUTE. WHY WOULD A RICH KID HAVE A PARTY AT THE PUBLIC PARK?
THERE'S A REASON THEIR PARENTS ARE RICH, ECHO. THEY MAKE SMART DECISIONS WITH THEIR MONEY.
WHY SPEND IT ON A PARTY VENUE WHEN YOU CAN GIVE AWAY EXPENSIVE GAMING CONSOLES TO STRANGE CHILDREN?
X BLOCKS
X BLOCKS
GO, GO, GO!

I *KNEW* IT WAS A SETUP!
THEN WHY DIDN'T YOU STOP ME?!

THOUGHT IT'D BE MORE FUN TO WATCH KARMA IN ACTION.

PSHOOOOOO

THIS IS BAD, JAMES! NOW THE GHOSTS HAVE COME BACK TO HAUNT ME TOO!

TIME TO PAY FOR RIPPING US OFF ON OUR BIRTHDAYS!

COME ON, NO ONE GOT "RIPPED OFF." WE DIDN'T VIOLATE THE GIFT FOR GOODIE BAG AGREEMENT!
I EVEN BROUGHT ONE TODAY!

SEE? IT DOESN'T HAVE TO . . .

IT'S *EMPTY!*

GUESS I SHOULD HAVE EXPECTED THAT, THIS BEING A SETUP AND ALL.

THIS ISN'T A GIFT, THIS IS GARBAGE!

SPRING UNDER TENSION CATAPULT RISK
SLANKY

YOU SAID YOU WERE GETTING A GOOD GIFT!
GOOD ENOUGH TO SAVE OUR BACON!

Ka-BWANG

Ka-BWONG
BACON? I'M STILL WAITING FOR LEMONADE!

TEAR

GO, GO, GO, GO!

baWHOOOM

MAN, SOME PARTY.

SLAP

WHUMP

PLEASE! DON'T HAUNT ME!
I WAS ONLY DOING IT BECAUSE MY BEST FRIEND MADE IT SEEM LIKE WE WOULDN'T GET *CAUGHT!*

GAH! IT *BURNS!*
WHY DO COTTON BALLS *BURN?!?!*

WHAT KIND OF—
OH, YOU DON'T WANT THAT. IT REALLY IS *GARBAGE.*

SO STICKY IT'LL TAKE A SURGEON TO REMOVE IT
89 CENTS

NO, NO, NO. THIS *IS* A GREAT GIFT.

NO, PLEASE.

I DIDN'T VIOLATE THE AGREEMENT!!!

MMAMAMHAHS.
GEEEETHTMDMDING!

WHAT'S THAT? I CAN'T UNDERSTAND YOU.
WELL, AT LEAST SOMETHING GOOD CAME OUT OF ALL THIS.

HEY! WHERE YOU GUYS GOING?
THIS GHOST WON'T STOP *HAUNTING ME!*
THE END

DEATH DAY AFTERNOON
Bucket List
Tom 22 Rogers

AND THEN WHAT DID YOU TELL HER?
IT'S MY MOM, MAX. I'M NOT AFRAID TO TELL HER THAT PLAYING HOCKEY INSIDE IS A GREAT WAY TO EXERCISE.

AHAHAHAHAHAHAHA!

JAMES, THIS TIME WE CAUGHT YOU DOING IT ON VIDEO!

REC
HONEY, DON'T LEAVE YOUR DIRTY DISHES IN THE SINK.

REC
WHIRRRRR
CRUNCH

WELL, THAT'S NOT ALL BAD. AT LEAST NOW WE KNOW WHY WE GO THROUGH GARBAGE DISPOSALS SO FAST.
YOU INVADED MY PRIVACY BY RECORDING ME WITHOUT MY PERMISSION?!

THAT'S LIKE ENTRAPMENT!
IT'S NOTHING LIKE ENTRAPMENT, HONEY. NO ONE *TOLD* YOU TO DESTROY THE DISHES.

YOU SAID YOU DIDN'T WANT TO SEE ANY DIRTY DISHES IN THE SINK!
AND DON'T CHANGE THE SUBJECT!
WHY IS IT THAT KIDS HAVE NO RIGHT TO PRIVACY?

BECAUSE THEY HAVE A PATTERN OF SOMETIMES DOING THINGS THAT MAY CAUSE THEMSELVES OR OTHERS HARM?
IS THAT REALLY A JUSTIFIABLE REASON TO ASSUME YOU CAN JUST *SPY* ON THEM?
YES. COMPLETELY.

WELL! IF YOU THINK VIOLATING THE SANCTITY OF THE KITCHEN WITH A HIDDEN CAMERA IS THE WAY TO TEACH ME A LESSON, YOU'VE SUCCEEDED . . .
SEE, THAT WASN'T SO BAD.

CRACK
SHOVE
. . . BECAUSE I'VE LEARNED THAT MY PARENTS HAVE *NO RESPECT* FOR *PRIVACY!*
BANG
CRASH
CLANG
OW! MY HUMERUS!

WHY DO THEY EVEN CALL IT THAT? IT'S NOT FUNNY AT ALL.

CAN YOU BELIEVE THEM, MAX? JUST BECAUSE THEY BIRTHED AND GAVE ME THE MIRACLE OF LIFE, THEY THINK THEY CAN DO WHATEVER THEY WANT!
WHY ARE YOU SO UPSET ABOUT BEING WATCHED BY YOUR PARENTS?

MY PARENTS ARE *ALWAYS* WATCHING ME. THAT JUST MEANS THEY CARE!

HI, MOM!

I TOLD YOU, MAXIMILIAN.
FOR THE SAKE OF THE EXPERIMENT, I'M NOT ALLOWED TO INTERACT WITH YOU.
OKAY, MOM!

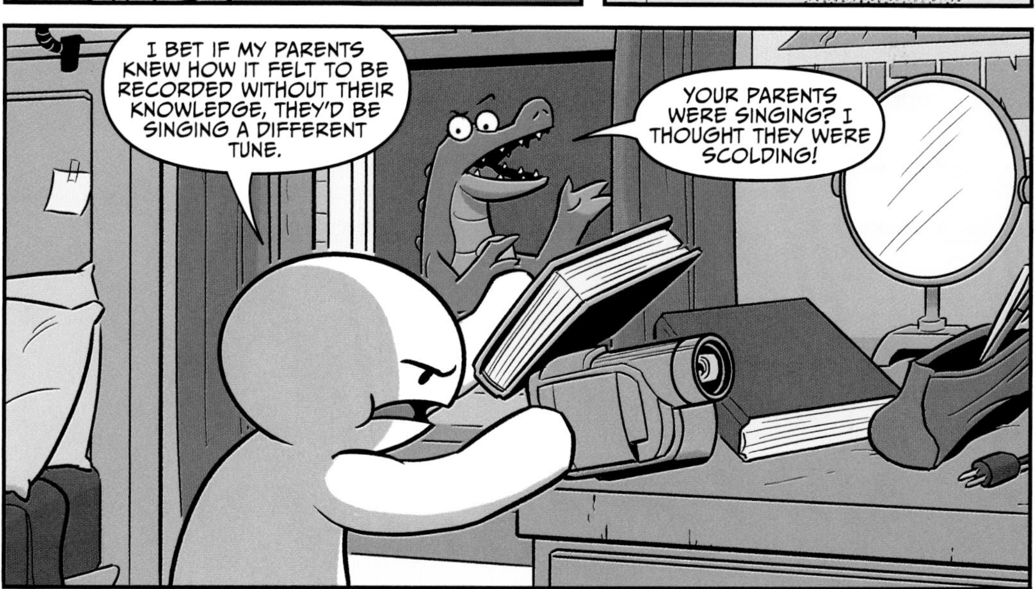
I BET IF MY PARENTS KNEW HOW IT FELT TO BE RECORDED WITHOUT THEIR KNOWLEDGE, THEY'D BE SINGING A DIFFERENT TUNE.
YOUR PARENTS WERE SINGING? I THOUGHT THEY WERE SCOLDING!

MOM? CAN I GET MY EARS CHECKED?

ACCORDING TO THE MULTIPLE DIAGNOSTIC TRACKERS EMBEDDED INSIDE YOU, YOUR HEARING IS COMPLETELY NORMAL.
THANKS, MOM!

SQUELCH!

THANKFULLY I'M MADE OF NOUGAT, SO THEY DIDN'T HEAR ANYTHING.

NOW, WHERE TO HIDE THE CAMERA . . .
I KNOW!

CRACK!

JAMES? BUDDY, THAT YOU?
WHAT ARE YOU *DOING?!*

NOW YOU CAN PUT THE CAMERA ANYWHERE BECAUSE YOUR PARENTS WILL BE LOOKING AT THE BROKEN TV.
HUH. SMART.

GO, GO, GO!
Snag!

HUH. THE TV'S BROKE.

YOU LET A BIRD IN AGAIN?

BIP

LIVE CAMERA FEED
MAYBE A CROW?
NO.

COULDA BEEN A SPARROW. THEY'RE SMALL. MAYBE YOU DIDN'T SEE IT?
IT WASN'T A *BIRD,* PATRICK!

JEEZ, LOUISE. I'M NOT SURE WHY YOU'RE SO RESISTANT TO MY BIRD THEORY.
BECAUSE IT WAS OUR SON. OUR SON WHO WON'T TAKE RESPONSIBILITY FOR ANYTHING.
THIS *JAMES EXPERIMENT* IS A *COMPLETE FAILURE.*

WELL, HANG ON. WE GOT SOME GOOD DATA.
YES, DATA THAT SAYS IT'S TIME TO CUT OUR LOSSES AND START OVER . . . AGAIN.

LIVE CAM
WHOA. WHOA. DO WE HAVE TO GO TO *THAT* EXTREME? I WAS STARTING TO LIKE THIS ONE.
PATRICK, THIS IS JUST LIKE ALL THE *OTHER* FAILED JAMES EXPERIMENTS.
AND IT'S TIME TO END THIS ONE *FOR GOOD.*

END IT? LIKE . . . END *ME?!*
BUT IT COULD HAVE BEEN A *BIRD!*

I CAN'T BELIEVE THIS. I'M JUST AN EXPERIMENT. LIKE *YOU.*

NO OFFENSE.
SOME TAKEN!

THEY APPARENTLY THINK I'M SUCH A FAILURE THAT THEY'RE GOING TO END ME!
THAT SEEMS EXTREME, EVEN FOR THEM.

APPARENTLY *NOT.*
DID YOU HEAR THEM? THIS ISN'T EVEN THE FIRST TIME! THERE HAVE BEEN OTHER JAMES EXPERIMENTS AND THEY ENDED *THEM* TOO!
MY LIFE . . . IS OVER!

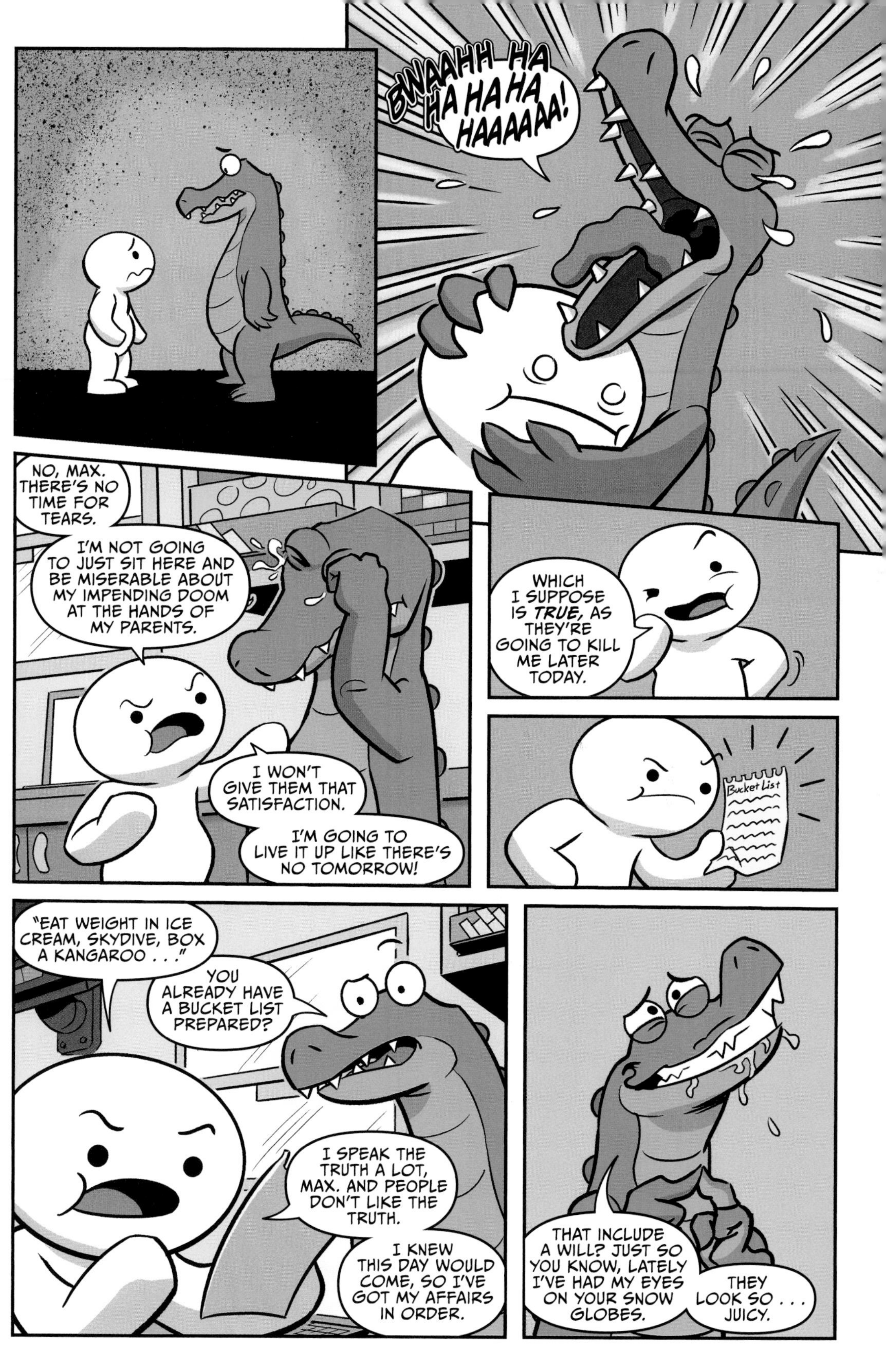
BWAAHH HA HA HA HA HAAAAAA!
NO, MAX. THERE'S NO TIME FOR TEARS.
I'M NOT GOING TO JUST SIT HERE AND BE MISERABLE ABOUT MY IMPENDING DOOM AT THE HANDS OF MY PARENTS.
WHICH I SUPPOSE IS *TRUE,* AS THEY'RE GOING TO KILL ME LATER TODAY.
I WON'T GIVE THEM THAT SATISFACTION.
I'M GOING TO LIVE IT UP LIKE THERE'S NO TOMORROW!
Bucket List
"EAT WEIGHT IN ICE CREAM, SKYDIVE, BOX A KANGAROO . . ."
YOU ALREADY HAVE A BUCKET LIST PREPARED?
I SPEAK THE TRUTH A LOT, MAX. AND PEOPLE DON'T LIKE THE TRUTH.
I KNEW THIS DAY WOULD COME, SO I'VE GOT MY AFFAIRS IN ORDER.
THAT INCLUDE A WILL? JUST SO YOU KNOW, LATELY I'VE HAD MY EYES ON YOUR SNOW GLOBES.
THEY LOOK SO . . . JUICY.

EXIT

IMPENDING DEATH IS SURPRISINGLY LIBERATING, MAX. I CAN OVERDOSE ON DAIRY WITHOUT WORRYING ABOUT GASTRIC DISTRESS!
Bucket List
•Eat the "Last Meal Special" at Dazed and Cone Fuzed

TEETER

MY BUDDY'S LAST MEAL ON A CONE!
IT'S OKAY, MAX. I'LL JUST CATCH IT ALL IN MY MOUTH LIKE YOU DO!

TOSS

SPLATT

LOOM!
PLEASE DON'T KILL ME IT'S MY PARENTS' FAULT. I WAS ONLY GETTING THE LAST MEAL SPECIAL BECAUSE THEY SAID THEY'RE GOING TO KILL ME!

YEAH, AND MY PARENTS' ARE GONNA TURN *ME* INTO GREEN GELATIN CUPS TO SERVE A PARTY OF TWELVE!
IT'S TRUE, WATCH!

PATRICK, THIS IS JUST LIKE ALL THE *OTHER* FAILED JAMES EXPERIMENTS. AND IT'S TIME TO END THIS ONE *FOR GOOD.*

YOU'RE AN EXPERIMENT?
LIKE *ME?*

WELL, I GUESS THERE'S NO USE PUMMELING YOU IF YOU'RE ALREADY GOING TO DIE.

BUT IF ANYONE ASKS YOU WHO DID YA IN, SAY IT WAS *ME!*

OH MAN! NOW YOU HAVE TO WAIT IN LINE ALL OVER AGAIN!
PUSH!

I WAS THINKING ABOUT THIS ALL WRONG, MAX. DYING IS EVEN BETTER THAN I THOUGHT.
OH, SO YOU'RE IN THE DENIAL STAGE!
OR IS IT THE BARGAINING STAGE?

THINK ABOUT IT, MAX. WHO'S GOING TO PUNISH A KID WHO'S AT HIS LIFE'S END?
IF STUART LET ME GET AWAY WITH THAT INFRACTION, I BET I CAN GET AWAY WITH ANYTHING!
Grieving for Gators CROCS

WHERE ARE YOU KEEPING ALL THIS PAPER?

Things I'd Do If I Knew I Was Going To Die
• Make throwing gum on sidewalk a major crime
• Ban passion fruit iced tea
• Rick Roll the city

UH, SOME OF THESE THINGS MIGHT MAKE PEOPLE MAD. LIKE, *MURDEROUSLY* MAD.
ESPECIALLY THAT MAGICIAN ONE. AND THEY CAN MAKE YOU DISAPPEAR!
IT'S OKAY, MAX. I'M GOING TO DIE TONIGHT ANYWAY, SO I WON'T BE AROUND TO DEAL WITH THE CONSEQUENCES!
AW, I WISH I WAS DYING.
• Make slides slide-able without clothing.
AND NOW TO MAKE THIS SLIDE SLIDE-ABLE FOR PEOPLE LIKE *US*, WHO STICK TO SAID SLIDES BECAUSE WE DON'T WEAR *CLOTHES!*
Baby Oil
GLUP
GLUP
GLUP

BOOOOM!

SMASH!
CRASH!
Tinkle

MY LEEEASE!

HAHAHAHAHA!

PATRICK, THIS IS JUST LIKE ALL THE *OTHER* FAILED JAMES EXPERIMENTS.
AND IT'S TIME TO END THIS ONE *FOR GOOD.*

WELL, THAT'S A FIRST.
I FEEL BAD FOR YOU *AND* DISLIKE YOU AT THE SAME TIME.

grumble
gramble
grumble

•Use superpowers
for inane things
LAB B-3

LAB B-3
CAN YOU TELL ME WHERE TO FIND THE BATHROOM?
AND NOT ONE OF THOSE BLACKHOLE ONES. I DON'T WANT MY WASTE GOING TO OTHER DIMENSIONS!

YOU'RE RIGHT. I *CAN'T* LET THAT TOILET SEND OUR WASTE TO BE SOMEONE ELSE'S PROBLEM!
THAT'S THE *FIRST* THING I'M GOING TO DESTROY WITH MY POWER SUIT!

CLANK
WHUNK
SHUNK
CLONK

AND NOW TO PROVE SUPER-POWERS SHOULDN'T JUST BE USED FOR RESCUING PEOPLE.
HEY! YOU! STOP THAT!
COLA
SPFFTT!
BZZZT!
ZAPPP!
KZZZT!
fizzle
MY LIFE'S WORK!
I'M GOING TO—
PATRICK, THIS IS JUST LIKE ALL THE *OTHER* FAILED JAMES EXPERIMENTS. AND IT'S TIME TO END THIS ONE *FOR GOOD.*

• Show walking is overrated
SO MUCH BETTER THAN WALKING.

PATRICK, THIS IS JUST LIKE ALL THE OTHER FAILED JAMES EXPERIMENTS. AND IT'S TIME TO END THIS ONE FOR GOOD.

. . . AND FOODBALL JOE SAID HE WOULDN'T LET ANYONE EAT HIS FOOD IN NON-BALL FORM.
PFFT. HE WILL IF YOUR PARENTS ARE GOING TO DO YOU IN!
I'LL TELL YA, MAX. THIS DAY HAS BEEN AMAZING. IT'S LIKE I DON'T EVEN CARE ABOUT DYING ANYMORE.

•Play taser tag with strangers

mnch mnch mnch
ALL RIGHT, WE GOTTA CHOOSE TEAMS. I'LL LET YOU PICK FIRST.

UM, BUT THERE'S NO STRANGERS.
Tumble

OOO, MAYBE IF WE BANG OUR HEADS SO HARD WE FORGET EVER KNOWING EACH OTHER, WE CAN STILL PLAY!
OOO! AND I WON'T FEEL SO BAD WHEN YOU'RE *GONE FOREVER!*

WHO DO WE WANT? JAMES!
WHEN DO WE WANT HIM? NOW!
COME ON. SOUNDS LIKE WE'LL FIND SOME TEAMMATES IN THE PARK.

LOOK, MAX. THEY DON'T WANT ME TO GO EITHER. THEY'RE HAVING A VIGIL!
AWWWW. IS THAT WHY THEY'RE ROASTING MARSHMALLOWS THAT LOOK LIKE YOU?

FLAME'S GETTIN' LOW. SOMEONE THROW ANOTHER JAMES PICTURE ON THE FIRE!

YAAAAYY!
FOOOM!

THIS ISN'T A VIGIL CELEBRATING MY LIFE. THIS IS A VIGIL CELEBRATING MY *DEATH!*

HEY! YOU CAN'T CELEBRATE MY DEATH!
OH, LOOK WHO IT IS. THE MAN OF THE HOUR!

OR SHOULD I SAY, THE MAN OF ONLY A *FEW* HOURS.
TAP TAP

FOR ONCE, I'M ACTUALLY *SURPRISED* YOU WANT ME DEAD, STUART. YOU SEEMED TO FEEL FOR MY PLIGHT.
YEAH, BUT THEN I SAW HOW EVERYONE ELSE WAS ANNOYED WITH YOU, AND FRANKLY I'M NOT GOOD WITH PEER PRESSURE, SO I'M CELEBRATING YOUR DEMISE.

WELL, I'M NOT GOING TO LET YOU USE MY DEATH AS AN EXCUSE TO PARTY!
SOMEONE DYING IS NOT A TOOL FOR *ENJOYMENT!*
BUT HAVEN'T *YOU* BEEN USING IT TO ENJOY DOING THINGS PEOPLE WOULD NORMALLY STOP YOU FROM DOING?

NOT NOW, MAX!

UM, SO WE'RE NOT STAYING FOR MARSHMALLOWS?
NO, MAX. WE'RE GOING HOME TO CONVINCE MY PARENTS NOT TO "END" ME SO I CAN SHOVE MY LIVING IN ALL OF THESE PEOPLE'S SMUG, MARSHMALLOW-EATING FACES!

OH.
OKAY.
Shmallows

Shmallows
YOINK

WAIT, BUT TO GET YOUR PARENTS NOT TO END YOUR LIFE, YOU'LL HAVE TO TAKE RESPONSIBILITY FOR YOUR SELF-CENTERED ACTIONS.
YEP. AND THE BEST PART IS, BY THE TIME I'M DONE OWNING UP, MY PARENTS WILL HAVE REALIZED THAT RESPECTING MY PRIVACY IS A MUCH BETTER WAY TO GO!

YOU REALLY GOING TO OWN UP TO ALL OF THEM?
WELL, ALL OF THEM EXCEPT THE ONE THEY HAVE VIDEO EVIDENCE OF ME DOING. THAT WAS AN INVASION OF PRIVACY.

NEW! HD!!
SET UP YOUR NEW TV

HOIST

TOSS!
CRASH!

JAMES!
HANG ON, MOM. BEFORE YOU DO ANYTHING LIFE-ALTERING TO ME, JUST GIVE ME FIVE MINUTES.

I'M HERE TO TAKE RESPONSIBILITY FOR MY ACTIONS.
BUT NOT THE TV, THAT WAS MAX.
B'P!
I'M HERE ABOUT THE ONES YOU DON'T EVEN *KNOW* ABOUT!

THERE WAS A HOME OFFICE INCIDENT.
AFTER I RANTED ABOUT MOM'S PRINTING LIMITATIONS AND TRIED TO REPLACE THE INK CARTRIDGES WITH FOOD COLORING.
CLK!

CLK!

BUT IT LOOKS FINE.
JUST A BACKDROP, DAD.

RIP!

MAYBE *THAT'S* HOW THE BIRD GOT IN.

REMEMBER THE TIME I ARGUED MY ROOM WASN'T FULL OF TRASH, BUT THAT I WAS COMPOSTING TO SAVE THE PLANET?
CLK!
YOU WERE *RIGHT,* AND IT CAUSED A RAT INFESTATION.

SO I ADDED CATS, BUT THEN *THAT* BECAME AN INFESTATION. I KEPT GOING UP THE PREDATOR FOOD CHAIN AND EVENTUALLY MADE LIONS SENTIENT SO I COULD *TRICK* THEM INTO MOVING INTO THE ZOO.
OH SWEET GEEFUS.

REMEMBER WHEN I RANTED ABOUT MOVIE-SHOP-PING MONTAGES NOT POSSIBLY BEING THAT FUN IN REAL LIFE?

I WENT ON A SHOPPING SPREE AND BOUGHT A SERIES OF RIDICULOUS OUTFITS THAT MAX KEPT SHAKING HIS HEAD "NO" AT.
CLK!

THIS WENT ON UNTIL WE MAXED OUT YOUR CREDIT CARDS.
BUT YOU SAID IT WAS CREDIT CARD FRAUD BY A GANG OF DIABOLICAL MOTHMEN IN NEED OF FOOD!

SORRY, DAD.
MAN, SOMEONE SHOULD PROBABLY CALL THE JAIL.
I PRESSED CHARGES. I THINK THOSE MOTHS GOT LIFE.

IS THERE A *POINT* TO THIS, OTHER THAN TO EMBARRASS AND ENRAGE US BY HOW BLIND WE'VE BEEN TO YOUR WILES?
YES. THE POINT IS, THIS IS WHY YOU *SHOULDN'T* INVADE MY PRIVACY.
NOT JUST BECAUSE IT'S A BASIC HUMAN RIGHT, BUT BECAUSE YOUR LIFE IS MUCH LESS STRESSFUL WHEN YOU DON'T KNOW ALL THE THINGS I'M DOING.

SO YOUR "TAKING RESPONSIBILITY" IS BASICALLY CONVINCING US . . . THAT IGNORANCE IS BLISS?
YES. AND THAT, IN A NUTSHELL, IS WHY YOU SHOULDN'T KILL ME.

YOU MEAN IN, LIKE, A METAPHORICAL SENSE?
NO, ACTUAL, UN-REVERSIBLE DEATH.
I RECORDED YOU ON A HIDDEN CAMERA TO SHOW YOU WHAT IT FEELS LIKE TO HAVE YOUR PRIVACY VIOLATED, AND HEARD YOU SAY YOU WERE GOING TO END THE JAMES EXPERIMENT.

HAHAHAHAHAHA!
OH, PAL. YOUR MOM WASN'T TALKING ABOUT ACTUALLY *KILLING* YOU.

YOU WEREN'T, RIGHT?

NO. OF COURSE NOT.

BUT WHAT ABOUT ALL THE OTHER JAMESES?!
YEAH, YOU SAID YOU'VE ENDED A *BUNCH* OF JAMES EXPERIMENTS!

YES, EXPERIMENTS WHERE WE'VE TRIED TO GET YOU TO ACCEPT RESPONSIBILITY FOR YOUR ACTIONS.
NOT OTHER JAMES EXPERIMENTS. THANKFULLY, THERE'S ONLY *ONE* OF YOU.

YES! I'M GOING TO LIVE!

HEY, WHERE ARE YOU GO—

JUST LET THEM GO, HONEY. I CAN'T HANDLE ANOTHER SLIDE SHOW.

DO YOU REALLY NEED TO DO THIS, JAMES? ISN'T TEACHING YOUR PARENTS ABOUT PRIVACY ENOUGH?
I HAVE TO FLAUNT BEING ALIVE, MAX. IT'S THE LAST ITEM ON MY LIST!

HOW DID I NOT SEE THAT BEFORE?!?
•Disappoint the entire town by not dying

MOM, CAN I GET MY EYES CHECKED?

HELLO, EVERYONE. YOU'LL BE UNHAPPY TO HEAR THAT I'M *NOT* GOING TO DIE!

WHAT?
NO WAY!
YOU'RE KIDDING!
YOU LIED TO US?!

WHAT?
YOU WERE DOING ALL THOSE STUPID THINGS, AND YOU GUILTED US INTO LETTING YOU GO 'CUZ YOU SAID YOU WERE DYING.
BUT YOU WEREN'T! YOU LIED!

YEAH!
LIAR!
EAT HIM!
EAT HIM?
HE'S NOT ONE OF THOSE *MARSHMAL-LOWS?*

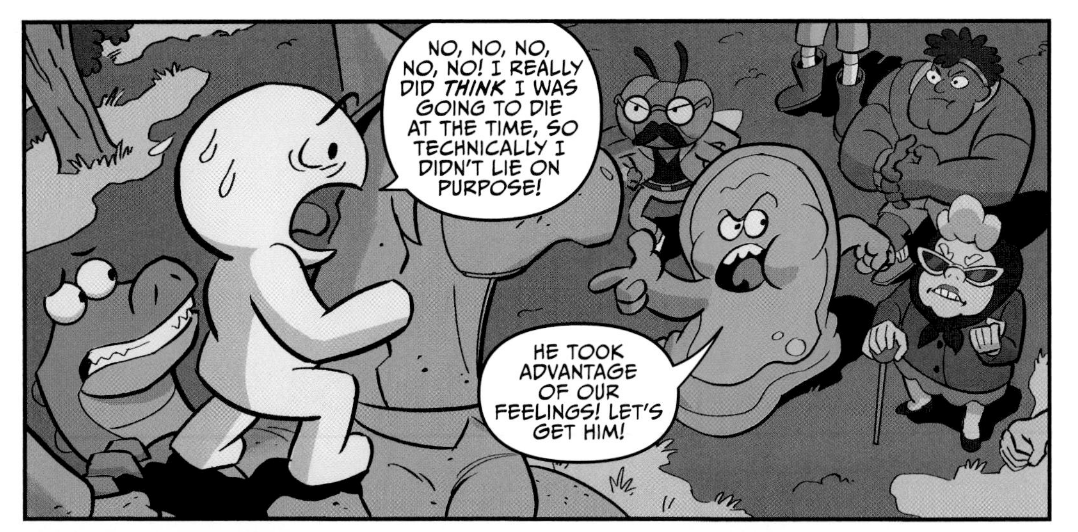
NO, NO, NO, NO, NO! I REALLY DID *THINK* I WAS GOING TO DIE AT THE TIME, SO TECHNICALLY I DIDN'T LIE ON PURPOSE!
HE TOOK ADVANTAGE OF OUR FEELINGS! LET'S GET HIM!

MAX, I'VE *SLIGHTLY* MISCALCULATED THE TOWN'S REACTION.

SHOW THEM THE VIDEO AGAIN! IF THEY THINK YOU'RE DYING, THEY'LL STOP!
JUST *RUN*, MAX!

BANG BANG BANG
MOM, DAD, LET ME IN!

SORRY, HONEY. WE'RE RESPECTING YOUR PRIVACY.

!!!

TO ROUGHAGE RIDGE!

JAMES!

AWWWW.
BOOO!
I'M STILL HUNGRY!

FLOAT
WE CAN STILL GET HIM!!!

KZZAP!!

Sizzle
FIZZLE
POP!

OOOOO!!!!!
AHHHHH!!!!
HE WAS A MARSHMAL-LOW!

WELL, JAMES, YOU WERE A HORRIBLE PERSON . . .

BUT A GOOD FRIEND.
SNIFF

JAMES! YOU'RE ALIVE?!

LIKE I SAID, MAX. I ALWAYS KNEW THIS COULD HAPPEN, SO I HAD A FAKING-MY-OWN-DEATH PLAN IN PLACE.

WAIT. HOW ARE YOU GOING TO GO ON LIVING IF YOU CAN'T LET ANYONE KNOW YOU'RE *ALIVE?*
DON'T WORRY, MAX. I'VE GOT A PLAN FOR THAT TOO.

"THOSE CLOTHES I BOUGHT TO TEST OUT MY MOVIE-MONTAGE THEORY WILL PROVIDE A GREAT DISGUISE."

I BET YOU'RE WONDERING WHY I'M SUDDENLY, FOR THE FIRST TIME, WEARING CLOTHES.
LET ME GIVE YOU A HINT—IT'S *NOT* BECAUSE YOU ASKED ME SEVENTY-SIX TIMES TO DO SO.

SORRY, PAL. BUT YOUR MOM SAYS WE DON'T WANT TO KNOW.
THAT'S RIGHT, HONEY. WE'RE RESPECTING YOUR PRIVACY.
NOW GO DO THE DISHES.

WHIRRR
GRIND
CRUNCH
THE END

ACKNOWLEDGMENTS

Like most creations, it took an amazing team of artists and humans to get us here. We'd like to thank our agent, Tim Travaglini, for creating this opportunity with TarcherPerigee, and our amazing editor, Lauren Appleton. A special thanks to Michael Zoumas, without whom we would never have met, and in turn *Oddballs* would not have been created. We'd also like to thank Netflix for letting us do whatever stories we wanted in this graphic novel, which we filled with all the stories that did not make it into the show.